UNDERSTANDING
EDMUND WHITE

UNDERSTANDING CONTEMPORARY AMERICAN LITERATURE
Matthew J. Bruccoli, Founding Editor
Linda Wagner-Martin, Series Editor

Volumes on
Edward Albee | Sherman Alexie | Nelson Algren | Paul Auster
Nicholson Baker | John Barth | Donald Barthelme | The Beats
Thomas Berger | The Black Mountain Poets | Robert Bly | T. C. Boyle
Raymond Carver | Fred Chappell | Chicano Literature
Contemporary American Drama | Contemporary American Horror Fiction
Contemporary American Literary Theory
Contemporary American Science Fiction, 1926–1970
Contemporary American Science Fiction, 1970–2000
Contemporary Chicana Literature | Robert Coover | Philip K. Dick
James Dickey | E. L. Doctorow | Rita Dove | John Gardner | George Garrett
Tim Gautreaux | John Hawkes | Joseph Heller | Lillian Hellman
Beth Henley | James Leo Herlihy | John Irving | Randall Jarrell
Charles Johnson | Diane Johnson | Adrienne Kennedy | William Kennedy
Jack Kerouac | Jamaica Kincaid | Etheridge Knight | Tony Kushner
Ursula K. Le Guin | Denise Levertov | Bernard Malamud | David Mamet
Bobbie Ann Mason | Colum McCann | Cormac McCarthy | Jill McCorkle
Carson McCullers | W. S. Merwin | Arthur Miller | Lorrie Moore
Toni Morrison's Fiction | Vladimir Nabokov | Gloria Naylor
Joyce Carol Oates | Tim O'Brien | Flannery O'Connor | Cynthia Ozick
Suzan-Lori Parks | Walker Percy | Katherine Anne Porter | Richard Powers
Reynolds Price | Annie Proulx | Thomas Pynchon | Theodore Roethke
Philip Roth | May Sarton | Hubert Selby, Jr. | Mary Lee Settle | Neil Simon
Isaac Bashevis Singer | Jane Smiley | Gary Snyder | William Stafford
Robert Stone | Anne Tyler | Gerald Vizenor | Kurt Vonnegut | David Foster
Wallace | Robert Penn Warren | James Welch | Eudora Welty
Edmund White | Tennessee Williams | August Wilson | Charles Wright

UNDERSTANDING

EDMUND
WHITE

Nicholas F. Radel

The University of South Carolina Press

© 2013 University of South Carolina

Published by the University of South Carolina Press
Columbia, South Carolina 29208

www.sc.edu/uscpress

Manufactured in the United States of America

22 21 20 19 18 17 16 15 14 13   10 9 8 7 6 5 4 3 2 1

Library of Congress Cataloging-in-Publication Data

Radel, Nicholas F., 1955–
  Understanding Edmund White / Nicholas F. Radel.
    p. cm.— (Understanding contemporary American literature)
  Includes bibliographical references and index.
  ISBN 978-1-61117-136-5 (hardcover : alk. paper) 1. White, Edmund,
  1940—Criticism and interpretation. I. Title.
  PS3573.H463Z84 2013
  813'.54—DC23   2012033263

*This book was printed on a recycled paper with 30 percent
postconsumer waste content.*

For Charles R. Forker

CONTENTS

SERIES EDITOR'S PREFACE

The Understanding Contemporary American Literature series was founded by the estimable Matthew J. Bruccoli (1931–2008), who envisioned these volumes as guides or companions for students as well as sophisticated non-academic readers, a legacy that will continue as new volumes are developed to fill in gaps among the nearly one hundred volumes published to date, embracing a host of new writers only now making their marks on our literature.

As Professor Bruccoli explained in his preface to the volumes he edited, because much influential contemporary literature makes special demands, "the word *understanding* in the titles was chosen deliberately. Many willing readers lack an adequate understanding of how contemporary literature works; that is, of what the author is attempting to express and the means by which it is conveyed." Aimed at fostering this understanding of good literature and good writers, the criticism and analysis in the series provide instruction in how to read certain contemporary writers—explicating their material, language, structures, themes, and perspectives—and facilitate a more profitable experience of the works under discussion.

In the twenty-first century, Professor Bruccoli's prescience gives us an avenue to publish expert critiques of significant contemporary American writing. The series continues to map the literary landscape and provide both instruction and enjoyment. Future volumes will seek to introduce new voices alongside canonized favorites, to chronicle the changing literature of our times, and to remain, as Professor Bruccoli conceived, contemporary in the best sense of the word.

Linda Wagner-Martin, Series Editor

ACKNOWLEDGMENTS

Many people deserve my thanks for helping bring this small book to completion. Professor Linda Wagner-Martin encouraged the project from the beginning, and the editorial staff at USC Press provided invaluable assistance throughout the writing. My colleagues on the Research and Professional Growth Committee at Furman University and Dean John Beckford supplied much needed collegial support and financial help for research travel and professional conferences associated with my work on White. The present and former chairs of the English department at Furman, Dr. Lynne Shackelford and Dr. Stanley Crowe, reconfigured the department's teaching schedule to give me time off to write the initial draft. I am also grateful to the trustees of Yale University and the staff at the Beinecke Rare Book and Manuscript Library for making Edmund White's papers available to me. The Beinecke librarians were extremely gracious in helping me sort through the voluminous material in that collection.

Edmund White generously provided me a copy of *Jack Holmes and His Friend* before the novel appeared in print and consented to be interviewed about his work with autobiography and biography. The necessarily abbreviated version of that interview in the present volume reflects only part of the immense range of White's brilliant commentary on that hot summer day, but what he taught me has, I hope, improved the work overall. White's partner, Michael Carroll, welcomed me into their home and provided me difficult to obtain copies of White's play, *Terre Haute*.

Perhaps no one has been more encouraging and supportive of my writing in American Studies than Magdalena J. Zaborowska at the University of Michigan; her enduring (though not necessarily warranted) faith has been my best inspiration over the years. Vincent Hausmann and Richard Letteri at Furman as well as Mario DiGangi at CUNY are always available to help me think through ideas. And John Antosca's technological know-how in helping me record, retrieve, and save the material from my interview with White was a godsend.

Finally, but no less urgently, I thank Luciano Desouza for his friendship and companionship. More than anything, his patience and good humor have sustained me throughout the writing of this book.

CHAPTER ONE

Understanding Edmund White

A significant coincidence is key to understanding Edmund White's fiction: his life as a gay man and his writing career developed simultaneously with the rise of a modern gay subculture in America and Europe. White came of age in the post–World War II era, when homosexuality was stigmatized and widely viewed as criminal. It was a time when gay men and women could not socialize in public, for people known to be or suspected of being homosexual could lose their jobs, run into trouble with the law, or be referred to dehumanizing medical treatment. Newspapers and magazines reported on homosexuality primarily as a type of social deviance or criminal behavior. There were no television shows about gay and lesbian people, and the few movies produced made them seem frightening and their lives shameful. Sensationalist pulp fiction novels about a largely imaginary underworld of gay life were published, but only a handful of novels written by or about gay men and lesbians could be considered serious, aesthetically important works. At best, gay men and women were thought to suffer from a psychological disorder, and while the founder of modern psychoanalysis, Sigmund Freud, had recommended tolerance, and suggested they be treated primarily to help them adjust to their stigmatized place in society, few American psychologists or psychoanalysts in the era of White's youth were so sanguine. Many, perhaps most, continued to advocate treatment for homosexuality itself.

During the 1960s and 1970s, however, when White began to write his novels, plays, and stories, attitudes began to change. African Americans and other minorities had been demanding greater equality in social and economic opportunities, and women struggled for gender equity. Gay men and women were also agitating for change in social attitudes and the law, starting as early as the 1950s, and in 1969 their efforts coalesced into a clear social movement, after a demonstration or minor riot occurred when police raided the Stonewall Inn, a gay bar in New York's Greenwich Village. That demonstration seemed to many—including White—to mark a symbolic turning point, and in the 1970s gay men and lesbians, particularly in large cities in the United States, achieved a high degree of social cohesion that allowed for new ways of seeing themselves as well as increased social and political power. Since the 1970s, gay and lesbian artists, intellectuals, and activists have helped bring about a sea change in American attitudes toward homosexuality, one in which gay people, as one of White's characters puts it, came to "constitute a community rather than a diagnosis."[1]

If this social progress was temporarily blunted by the emergence of AIDS in the 1980s and 1990s, in the twenty-first century gay men and women are living openly in America, seeking full civil rights and functioning as productive citizens within American democracy. White's novels and short stories record—and indeed were perhaps a "catalyst to"—these changes.[2] Their dominant themes include the self-doubt his gay characters experience as they grow into adults during the 1950s and 1960s in America and their sometimes difficult emergence into the new worlds they were helping to create in the 1970s and later. White's fiction combines a devastating critique of American sexual hypocrisy with a shrewd analysis of the perils and progress of, especially, white middle-class, gay male lives.

Still, it is not the political or social content of his work that makes White so singularly important; it is that he writes fiction of the highest artistic order. His work is never simply political and rarely polemical. White's younger colleague, the novelist David Leavitt, was praising White when he wrote that his novels are answerable only to themselves, to the demands that make for good writing, and not particular political ideologies, gay or straight. His persistent artistic goal, Leavitt continued, is to create "a compelling fictional universe."[3] White's first published novel, *Forgetting Elena* (1973), was praised by no less a figure than Vladimir Nabokov. *A Boy's Own Story* (1982), his breakthrough autobiographical novel about growing up gay in the American Midwest, achieved a wide readership in America and abroad, and was praised for fitting "the classic mold of works exploring adolescent sexuality."[4] Writing in the *New York Times*, Christopher Lehmann-Haupt expressed what many feel: "this is not exclusively a homosexual boy's story. It is any boy's story. . . . For all I know, it may be any girl's own story as well."[5]

White reorients our understanding of homosexuality in American life by giving expression to it in the high literary modes that have traditionally been used to validate only heterosexual lives. In *The Beautiful Room Is Empty* (1988), White's narrator fears that, as a homosexual writer, he will "never be able to give a convincing account of marriage, birth, parental love, conjugal intimacy, the spicy anguish of adultery—none of the great occasions" (148). But if the insecure young narrator feels that homosexual experience is too constrictive to be of value in producing art and literature, the whole of White's work contests that idea by showing how gay experience itself is a source of great occasions and that gay fiction can stand alongside all the other important literary works that define and record America's history and culture.

Edmund Valentine White III was born on January 13, 1940, in Cincinnati, Ohio, a small, conservative midwestern city where he spent his childhood and significant portions of his adolescent life. His father was a chemical engineer who established a successful business selling industrial equipment. His mother, born Delilah Teddlie, spent the first years of her marriage as a housewife, but later trained as a child psychologist and for more than two decades ran a clinic for mentally handicapped children in the Chicago area. White's early years, then, were spent in middle-class affluence as a child of accomplished, if distant, parents. At age seven, however, his parents divorced, and his mother took him and his sister Margaret to Evanston, Illinois, outside Chicago. The experience left him feeling rejected by his powerful father, an emotion evoked over and over in his novels and stories. But it also left him, according to White's late nephew Keith Fleming, with a profound sense that individual lives could be radically changed, and that one could create oneself anew in a better world—ideas central to White's fiction.[6]

Precocious in a number of ways, White was actively seeking sex with other boys and even men by the time he was thirteen or fourteen,[7] when he first revealed his homosexuality to his mother in an outburst biographer Stephen Barber describes as "anguish[ed]" and "defiant."[8] The young novelist explored some of these feelings in *Dark Currents* (1955), his first novel, written when White was fifteen. Although it remains unpublished, *Dark Currents* shows White already exploring themes that recur in his mature fiction: the struggle of his protagonist, Peter Cross, with his sexuality and the conflict between erotic desire and friendship.[9] It was a courageous achievement for a young writer to tackle such themes so openly, and a highly original one considering how little precedent there was for the empathetic exploration of homosexuality in fiction. Nevertheless White's parents exchanged worried letters about their son's homosexuality, and it seems likely these worries played a part in the writer's being transferred during his high-school years to the Cranbrook Boys School outside Detroit, where, it was thought—obviously incorrectly—that a greater masculine influence would help him overcome his sexual orientation.

After graduating, White studied Chinese at the University of Michigan, where he took his degree in 1962. Scrapping plans to attend graduate school at Harvard, he moved instead to New York and became a staff writer at Time-Life Books. Almost immediately, White achieved a minor literary success when a play he had written at the University of Michigan, *The Blue Boy in Black*, was produced off-Broadway in spring 1963. It featured the then up-and-coming actors Cicely Tyson and Billy Dee Williams, and although it ran only thirty-two performances, the play was recognized as the work of a promising newcomer. *The Blue Boy in Black* tells the story of a talented black writer, Joan, and her struggle to succeed in a racially polarized America. According to one of White's best critics, David Bergman, Joan represents "White's first attempt to draw his version of the social psychology of oppression," one of his most important themes.[10] The play reflects as well White's misgivings about his own chances for success as a member of a sexual minority that had little opportunity to speak for itself in mainstream America. For even though White was writing autobiographical fictions throughout the 1960s and came close to publishing one of them in the 1970s, a novel called *Like People in History*, few publishers at the time were willing to take a chance on gay-themed works by unknown authors.[11]

White's literary career only began in earnest when he left Time-Life Books in 1970 and (ironically, considering his later successes in autobiographical fiction) turned away from realistic gay subject matter. The experimental *Forgetting Elena* is a satire of manners about a young man living in a highly sophisticated society who seems unable to remember even the most rudimentary things about himself, including who he is. White wrote it, he says, only to please himself, and when it was finally published in 1973, it was recognized as "a masterful piece of work."[12] If it is one of White's most difficult novels, it continues to be acclaimed as one of his best. Still, White was not able to make his living writing novels, and, as he details in his memoir *City Boy* (2009), he worked at different times in the 1970s as an editor both for *Horizon* and the *Saturday Review*. He also earned money ghost-writing college textbooks, teaching creative writing at Johns Hopkins and Columbia universities, and writing freelance essays and reviews for top magazines and newspapers. These occasional writings helped White establish himself as a masterful commentator on the arts and culture, a role he continues to play today. Many were later collected in *The Burning Library* (1994), *Arts and Letters* (2004), and *Sacred Monsters* (2011).

Despite his workaday obligations, the 1970s and early 1980s were still among the most important in White's creative career. White played a substantial role in helping create a new gay literary movement emerging in the 1970s that Robert McRuer has justly dubbed a "Queer Renaissance."[13] At this time, gay and lesbian authors began to write openly, to explore, as White puts it, "their own most intimate feelings," and "orient themselves in a world—the gay world—[they were] just beginning to map."[14] Although he continued to write autobiographical gay fictions that remain unpublished, another experimental work, *Nocturnes for the King of Naples* (1978), assured him a place in the history of gay male literature in America. An elegy of lost love and an anatomy of the mental state of the lover who loses it, *Nocturnes,* along with Andrew Holleran's *Dancer from the Dance* and Larry Kramer's *Faggots,* became one of three explicitly gay fictions published by mainstream American presses in a single year. Never before had the big American publishing houses taken a chance on the kinds of middle-class gay fictions White and his peers were writing. Others, especially minority writers such as Gloria Anzaldúa, the great James Baldwin, Randall Keenan, and Audre Lorde, were also helping bring about the renaissance in queer literature McRuer describes, but it seems fair to say that *Nocturnes* was significant in helping establish this new era of gay visibility in American letters.

What is more, at this point in his career White also played a key role in shaping public perception of the gay lifestyles emerging in cities across America. Two works of nonfiction made him something of a national spokes- man for white, urban gay men. In 1977, White co-authored, with psychiatrist Dr. Charles Silverstein, *The Joy of Gay Sex,* a work that explored in intimate detail the sexual practices, pleasures, and pains of gay men. Its nod to Alex Comfort's earlier groundbreaking book, *The Joy of Sex* (1972), boldly announced that gay lives and sex were as legitimate areas of emotional and legal concern as straight ones. (*The Joy of Lesbian Sex* appeared around this time as well.)

Even more important, in 1980 White published *States of Desire: Travels in Gay America,* a guide to the major centers of gay life in America in the 1970s. Despite being criticized for its numerous exclusions—the book con- centrates primarily on affluent, urban, white men—*States of Desire* helped define for many Americans the meanings of the social experiments in gay visibility, self-definition, and community taking place at the time. Reviewer Richard Goldstein remarked wittily in the *Village Voice* that "quite the best thing about *States of Desire,* its *modus eroticus,* if you will, is White's attempt to explain the most tangible aspects of gay culture to homosexuals, who may be more confused by what they do than heterosexuals are by what they see."[15] The book remains one of our most important nonfiction sources for understanding the white urban gay male subculture that emerged in America in the 1970s.

During this period as well, White was associated with a small informal convocation of gay writers in New York City that came to be called the Violet Quill. The group, which included Christopher Cox, Robert Ferro, Michael Grumley, Andrew Holleran, Felice Picano, and George Whitmore, was in the forefront of creating a specifically gay American fiction in the late 1970s and 1980s. These men's works "represent an early high watermark in gay writing,"[16] and their novels and stories helped give voice to a minority that had previously been much spoken about but that had not, until that point, done much speaking for itself. Not surprisingly, the dominant literary mode of the Violet Quill writers was autobiography, for as Bergman points out, "autobiographical fiction is the means that gay novelists have of 'telling their own story,' and in so doing, defying the homophobic stereotypes of the past and creating new myths for the future."[17]

White's association with the group marked a turning point in his career, because at this time he completed and succeeded in publishing his first auto-biographical novel, *A Boy's Own Story* (1982). Still, perhaps the Violet Quill did not so much influence White—he was, after all, writing gay auto-biographical fiction as early as the 1950s—as give him, and all its members, confidence in the belief "that they were writing specifically and openly for a gay readership which existed and would be receptive to their work."[18] While not referring directly to the Violet Quill writers, White in *City Boy* suggests, no doubt correctly, that the explicit, autobiographical gay literature he and others were producing not only shaped an audience but created an under-standing of what it means to be gay: "After centuries of oppression we had a sense of community we wanted to celebrate in novels that would create our identity while also exploring it."[19]

Although White produced another of his dense, stylistically baroque works, *Caracole*, in 1985, he became less interested in experimental meta-narratives after *A Boy's Own Story* and focused increasingly on auto-biographical, even biographical fictions. He conceived a plan to write a series of four autobiographical novels that would cover gay life in America in each decade from the 1950s through the 1980s, but, in the event, produced a trilogy instead. *A Boy's Own Story* was followed by *The Beautiful Room Is Empty,* an account of his narrator's life in New York in the 1960s, and nearly a decade later by *The Farewell Symphony* (1997), which continued the story of White's narrator into the 1990s. White changed his plans in part because he decided the contrast between the sexually open 1970s and the bleak AIDS years of the 1980s would more effectively represent the shape of gay life in those decades.

But perhaps he had a more practical reason as well. In 1985 White himself tested positive for HIV, and he feared he would not live long enough to fulfill his original ambition. With his usual courage, White made his diagnosis public as a way of combating the fear and shame associated with the disease at that time. But even though he is one of the extremely rare people in whom the disease does not progress quickly, and he has lived well into the era when HIV infection can be more effectively controlled with drugs, White's fears about his future seemed real enough at the time.

In the 1980s, White helped found the Gay Men's Health Crisis, a grass-roots social service agency in New York City that continues to provide education in safe-sex practices and support for people with HIV infection today. Typically, however, his primary response to AIDS was literary. Early on, White wrote two short stories, "An Oracle" and "Palace Days," that were among the first examples of a new genre of AIDS fiction and first collected in *The Darker Proof* (1987), which White produced along with British writer Adam Mars-Jones. Both writers agreed that the short story was, initially at least, the appropriate form to explore the new disease. "The novel," White said, "has an inevitable trajectory to it. That is, you begin healthy and end sick and dead. We wanted to get into and out of the subject matter in a more angular and less predictable way."[20]

The result was a brilliant, often fragmentary style of short fiction that reveals the disruption the disease causes in its characters' lives even as it provides a "personal and subjective" focus on their struggles. "We were trying to remind people that it was actual, thinking and feeling human beings who were living through this."[21] In a later collection, *Skinned Alive* (1995), White published additional stories, many about AIDS, that some critics see as being among his best works. Still, he could not for long defer exploring the disease in the novel, even if that form, at least in part, reproduces what White says seemed like "the inevitable trajectory" of AIDS. Both *The Farewell Symphony* and *The Married Man* (2000) reflect White's life with his then partner, Hubert Sorin, a young Frenchman who died of AIDS in 1994. But, as in the stories, the novels' focus on the lives rather than the deaths of their characters gives them great humanity.

A second important change in White's life occurred nearly simultaneously with the publication of *A Boy's Own Story*. In 1983, using money he received from the Guggenheim Foundation to complete work on *Caracole*, White moved to Paris where he spent the next fourteen years. White had

lived in Rome briefly in the early 1970s, and he often summered in Venice in
the same decade—experiences reflected in the exotic settings of novels such
as *Nocturnes for the King of Naples* and *Caracole*. So, European culture and
life have always been a formative influence on White's work. But it was while
he was in Paris that White wrote his magisterial biography of the French
novelist and playwright Jean Genet. *Genet: A Biography* (1993) profoundly
affected his handling of later fiction—in particular *The Farewell Symphony*.
During this time as well White's fiction—especially those works set specifically outside America—began to participate in the venerable tradition,
descending from Henry James through James Baldwin and others, of exploring American cultural mores from a vantage point in Europe. One critic aptly
suggests that a source of White's strength as a commentator on gay American
lives derives in part from his being "deeply reliant on non-American cultures
in the construction of his fictions."[22]

Nevertheless in 1997 White returned from France to accept a position as
professor of English at Princeton University, where he teaches today. Since
his repatriation, White has turned to historical fiction. He wrote, first, *Fanny:
A Fiction* (2003), about the travels in America of two celebrated nineteenth-
century British women, Frances Trollope and Frances Wright, and followed
up with *Hotel de Dream: A New York Story* (2007), his fictional account of
the last days of the great American author Stephen Crane, who lived his last
years in England and died in Germany. White has also written a successful
drama, *Terre Haute* (2007), loosely based on prison interviews the novelist
Gore Vidal conducted with the Oklahoma City bomber, Timothy McVeigh.
Terre Haute premiered in Edinburgh in 2006 and toured the United Kingdom
in 2007. Its U.S. premier took place at the New Conservatory Theatre in San
Francisco in April 2007, and it opened in New York in 2009.[23]

Finally, inspired by his experience writing biographies—in addition to his
biography of Genet, he also wrote *Marcel Proust* (1999) and *Rimbaud: The
Double Life of a Rebel* (2008)—White has also started writing about his own
life in nonfiction forms. He has written both an autobiography, *My Lives*
(2005), and a memoir, *City Boy: My Life in New York During the 1960s and
'70s* (2009). But he has not abandoned his commitment to autobiographical
fiction, for in 2007 he published *Chaos,* another collection of tales linked in
some ways to his stories about AIDS by their emphasis on the degeneration
of the aging bodies of his protagonists and narrators. And in January 2012,
he published *Jack Holmes and His Friend*—a novel that spins variations on
the conventions of autobiographical realism for which White is most famous.

Over the past two decades White has merited a number of impressive
literary honors. For his biography of Genet, he won the National Book

Critics Circle Award as well as one of the highest honors for literary and artistic merit issued by the French government, the *Chevalier de L'Ordre des Arts et des Lettres*. In 1997, he became a member of the American Academy of Arts and Letters, and in 2010 was again honored by a national government when Italy awarded him its prestigious *Premio Letterario Internazionale Mondello* for his biography of Rimbaud. His life reflects the ways gay and lesbian people have moved from a despised, marginal place in American culture to a central one, and the quality of his work puts to rest any lingering doubts about the validity of gay and lesbian intellectuals and authors to occupy that place.

White's greatest achievement is to have helped create a literature that represents gay lives to an American reading public in middle-class terms. The very few novels about gay life that were written before the late 1960s in America "tried to create sympathy for homosexuality by depicting gay males as 'sad young men.'"[24] The new gay writing White was creating concerned "what happened to men from the middle class who identified as gay and who attempted to live their lives not in the closet but as gay men."[25] In the 1960s and 1970s, White says, "publishers were prepared to publish books like those by [John] Rechy or Jean Genet or William Burroughs about freaky people, drug-takers, pimps, prostitutes, marginal gay people. . . . But it was more threatening to write about a person who was really quite like the presumably middle-class reader, except that he happened to be gay."[26]

And yet, if White represents gay lives in terms that middle-class people—gay and straight—understand, his work decidedly does not call for the assimilation to middle-class sexual norms and social mores that some gay thinkers began to advocate in the years after the Stonewall Riots. Even in his early autobiographical novels, in which his narrators struggle with their conflicting desires both to be gay and to fit into the middle-class worlds into which they are born, White remains acutely aware that the kinds of sexual differences reflected in his gay characters were salutary antidotes to the sterile repressiveness he saw in middle-class America. His later work, too, seeks new ways of understanding sex and physical desire that are not limited to conventional norms of heterosexual society. And he can be critical as well of new gay moralities that attempt simply to reproduce dominant American lifestyles.[27]

Inevitably the complexity of White's social analysis has led critics to be divided over the significance of gay identity in his work. Some read White in relation to the identity-politics model of gay struggle for social acceptance while others find in his work an occasion to advance the queer, postgay, or postidentity understandings of subjectivity that became fashionable in the

1990s. White is clearly concerned with the ways his characters' lives are distorted by social homophobia, and his early gay novels in particular are about characters who cannot achieve a secure sense of identity or self because homosexuality remains an abject condition in American life.[28] In some ways, the early novels are types of gay coming-out stories that emphasize their individual gay characters' efforts to achieve self-respect and social acceptance as gay men. As such, they have come under attack.

Robert McRuer, for instance, criticizes White for what he sees as a singular focus on sexual oppression in *A Boy's Own Story*. According to McRuer, White does not take into sufficient account ways his white, middle-class (and we might add male) privilege insures that his experience of being gay differs from others'. To the extent that White's is a story of individual triumph over social adversity, it is "a suspiciously white and middle-class move toward 'self-respect,' not revolutionary social change."[29] In reading White, we do well to keep in mind McRuer's point that not all gay and lesbian Americans have been allowed to achieve individual self-esteem and self-respect or would necessarily consider these to be the main goals of their social struggle for rights in America. Still, it seems unfair to criticize White or his narrator for telling his own and not others' stories of struggle. David Bergman replies to McRuer by arguing that *A Boy's Own Story* records the specificities of its particular narrator's gay subject position, and readers with different racial, ethnic, gendered, or class positions will pick and choose aspects of that experience they wish to identify with or not.[30]

More recent critical work attempts to move beyond these arguments by examining White's novels in a postidentity framework that does not, in Tony Purvis's words, "assume that sexual subjectivity in America is a cultural or personal constant." Purvis argues that, rather than seeing homosexuality as an identity fixed in the individual subject, White's novels recognize gayness as "textual," an identification that always means differently within the discourses in which it is produced.[31] So, Purvis continues, rather than tell one version of what it means to be gay in America, White's novels reveal a multiplicity of ways. Finally, my own recent work suggests that gayness in at least one of White's novels is produced around the incoherencies of white racial identifications in twentieth-century American history, so that gay identity itself never achieves the kind of coherence that was widely assumed to be the goal of the identity-politics model that influenced White in his early years.[32]

What seems clear is that White is neither bound exclusively to the goal of liberating a gay identity seen as inherent within the individual nor to the poststructuralist goal of elaborating philosophically the textuality of all, including gay, identities. Because White's work meditates complexly on sexual difference in America, we can expect it to be open to interpretation from both—indeed many—angles. Les Brookes argues that White's work reflects a long tradition in writing about gay characters in the twentieth century that illustrates and accepts conflicting ideas about what it means to be gay in society. If the novels sometimes reveal a fascination with "gay identity and community," they also at times demonstrate their impatience with both.[33] Such identifications as we discover in White's fictions produce shifting understandings of gay identities and their relation to a society that continues to be uncomfortable about sex and same-sex attraction. What remains constant is the author's celebration of the way gay men in America created themselves out of and in relation to a homophobic society in the 1960s and beyond, a process that helped change that society. White's novels demonstrate the processes by which gay identities emerged in relationship to an oppressive homophobia dominant in American culture, and they hold forth gracefully on the possibilities for re-imagining oneself as well as society within the transformations of time, memory, and imagination.

CHAPTER TWO

White's Autobiographical Trilogy

A Boy's Own Story, The Beautiful Room Is Empty,
and *The Farewell Symphony*

Although White began his career as a novelist in earnest with the publication of the critically admired, experimental works *Forgetting Elena* (1973)
and *Nocturnes for the King of Naples* (1978), the trilogy of autobiographical novels he began writing in the late 1970s made him famous as part of
a small group of writers creating a new gay literature in the United States.
By some accounts he also helped create in the 1980s and 1990s what had
never existed before or perhaps after, a clearly identifiable audience for gay
writing. *A Boy's Own Story* (1982), *The Beautiful Room Is Empty* (1988),
and *The Farewell Symphony* (1997) are based on White's experience growing up in 1950s America in the Midwest and his coming of age as a gay man
in the 1970s and 1980s in New York and Paris. The trilogy begins with a
boy precocious enough even in adolescence to understand and act on his
desire for other males but who also accepts the negative cultural stereotyp-
ing of homosexuality he sees all around him—stereotypes that shape others'
responses to him and, worse, his response to himself. By the final novel of the
trilogy, however, he lives openly as a gay man within a community in New
York City that affirms the legitimacy of his sexual choices. Although that
life is overshadowed and ultimately transformed by AIDS, this community is
vibrant and creative, a world of artists and intellectuals that makes important
contributions to the cultural life of America as a whole and becomes a source
of power for consolidating and continuing the change in attitudes toward sex
and sexuality the novels record.

This story of change and transformation in gay people is fundamental in White's work, and so intertwined is the history of gay communities in the United States with the story of White's own personal growth as a gay man that in *The Farewell Symphony* the novelist is able to make light of his own autobiographical practice when his narrator claims to be writing a book that is "purely autobiographical. Everything in it is exactly as it happened, moment by moment—sometimes even written down moments after the event. . . . That's the avant-garde technique I've invented: it's called realism."[1] As we will see, this statement does not accurately describe White's novels, which artfully shape their material to highlight the author's interpretation of ideas and understanding of character. But it leads us to see what the narrator means when, later in the novel, he says that "hovering just over the divide between invention and reportage struck me as inherently interesting, especially when what was being reported was a whole new world of experience" (254). White suggests that one of his primary purposes as a writer is simply to tell what it was he saw happening in his life as a gay man in America, because that subject was, and remains, fascinating in itself.

The most important theme of White's trilogy may be that, by putting aside the self-hatred that derives from negative social attitudes toward homosexuality, gay men learned to esteem themselves in ways that led them into powerful, productive lives and strong social identifications. To cite *The Farewell Symphony* once again, White's narrator writes that "mutual love" depends on "self-esteem," so that for gay men to be able to love other gay men, to form useful associations and communities, they first had to learn to love themselves (29). The trilogy demonstrates with a great deal of perspicuity and attention to historical nuance the ways a particular group of white, middle-class gay men contributed to changes in postwar America by re-inventing and re-imagining themselves outside the negative stereotypes about homosexuality that dog White's young narrators. As such it belongs to the confessional tradition out of which much American multicultural literature arises. It helps provide a voice for a minority community that had, so far in American history, been ignored and overlooked.

The trilogy (and the individual novels of which it is comprised) seems to emerge from a specific gay cultural narrative, what is called in gay studies a "coming-out story." Coming out describes the process by which (usually young) gay and lesbian people learn to accept their sexual difference and understand how they will (and will not) address that difference in a social or public way. As a literary form, the coming-out novel tends to describe the transformation of the gay individual from a suppressed and closeted person into a liberated and happy one.[2] White has said that the success of *A Boy's Own Story* rests partially on the ways it "seemed to fill an empty niche in the contemporary publishing ecology, the slot of the coming-out novel,"[3] and his novel was one of the earliest to forge a literary structure for that particular gay coming-of-age theme. Throughout *A Boy's Own Story* and *The Beautiful Room Is Empty* we see the narrator struggling to come to terms with his emerging awareness of his sexuality in ways that will allow him to live life on his own terms. And if we read the earlier novels in relation to the last novel of the trilogy, we find further evidence for understanding the whole in terms of the coming-out narrative—for in *The Farewell Symphony* White's young narrator seems to have grown into a self-accepting adult who lives his life as a gay man in a public, unashamed way.

But as is true of nearly all efforts to fit complex works of art into the narrow slot of a specific genre, White's novels inhabit the form of the coming-out narrative only imprecisely.[4] Not one of White's three novels leaves its narrator with an unalloyed sense of happiness. *A Boy's Own Story* ends with its narrator performing a despicable act of sexual betrayal that imitates the abuses of adult sexual power he sees all around him. So the novel violates normative expectations for representing gay characters positively that were implicit in the usual structure of the coming-out novel. White has said as well that his "strategy in *The Beautiful Room Is Empty* was to present a gay hero so self-hating that even the most retrograde reader would become impatient with his inner torment."[5] This is precisely what the reviewer in *The New York Times* felt when he wrote that, "instead of wanting [the narrator] to find the 'cause' of and the 'cure' for his homosexuality, we find ourselves wearying of his search and wishing him simply to accept his desires."[6] And the presence of AIDS in *The Farewell Symphony* makes for a complex understanding of what it means for its characters to have achieved the sexual liberation that is so much the theme of the final novel of the trilogy.

More than a coming-out narrative, White's trilogy is a precise and highly analytical exploration of the sexual and social power relationships that define homosexuality and a particular group of gay men in America in the several decades after World War II. White is writing not simply about individual characters but a historical movement. "We learned," White has written, "that what we'd lived through was not a neurosis in need of treatment but a shared experience that called for political action."[7] It is in sociological terms that we can best understand the complexity of White's work without altogether ignoring the trilogy's celebration of the many positive changes in gay life from the 1950s through the 1990s that it reveals.

A Pathetic Malady: Self-Division in *A Boy's Own Story*
and *The Beautiful Room Is Empty*

A Boy's Own Story and *The Beautiful Room Is Empty* are not at all similar
works. But the two novels narrate the life of, presumably, the same nameless
young man, someone much like White himself, from his earliest memories of
childhood through his adolescence and early adulthood in New York. Name-
lessness is one device White uses to suggest that his narrator never achieves
a sure sense of belonging in his society by virtue of his precocious talent,
unconventional socialization, and—most significant of all—sexual difference
from other boys. One implication of the novels, especially when we read
them in connection with *The Farewell Symphony,* is that the narrator will
not be able to achieve any of these goals until he can think about society and
his relationship to it in new ways and thereby invent himself and his society
anew. Both *A Boy's Own Story* and *The Beautiful Room Is Empty* thematize
the "self division" of their narrators, that is, their inability to integrate their
sexual desires and experiences productively with the sexual and social values
of their society.[8] We might begin to understand them, then, by examining the
various aspects of their narrators' estrangement from themselves and society.

In *A Boy's Own Story,* this idea is perhaps nowhere clearer than in the
final scenes of the novel, when White's priggish narrator seduces a teacher at
his boarding school, Mr. Beattie, and then betrays him to the school authori-
ties. Ostensibly protecting the school he otherwise hates from the pernicious
influence of the hip, pot-smoking Beattie, the narrator smokes marijuana
with the teacher, reports him to the headmaster for drug violations, and
then returns to Beattie's office to have sex with him. It is a calculated and
despicable trap, for the narrator is aware that Beattie "wouldn't be able to
discredit me by saying I was a practicing homosexual since we would have
practiced homosexuality together. He'd be powerless."[9] The narrator's action
is a complex one that sums up many strands of White's thinking about the
interrelations between the social abjection of homosexuality and the narrator's individual psychology. His motive, the narrator says, is that he wanted
"to have sex with a man and then to disown him and it; this sequence was
the ideal formulation of [his] impossible desire to love a man but not to be
a homosexual" (218). The comment suggests that there is a difference in the
narrator's mind between the desire he feels for men and the social image of
homosexuality given him by his society, and that the narrator cannot reconcile the two. As the novel makes clear, there simply are no socially approved
ways for the narrator to understand his sexuality in 1950s America, and one
result of that lack is his repudiation of homosexuality, which leads to his

entrapment of Beattie and a symbolic betrayal of himself as a young homosexual man.

But White also sees the narrator in terms of the dysfunctions of adult
male sexuality evidenced throughout the novel. Perhaps most significant
about the scenes in which the narrator betrays Beattie, White represents his
protagonist's action as an attempt to gain a sense of control or power over
his own sexual acts and sexuality. In the closing lines of the novel, the narrator seems pleased with his betrayal and smugly reports that "I who had so
little power . . . had at last drunk deep from the adult fountain of sex" (218).
He sees himself as imitating the actions of others, especially but not only adult
men who use sex to assert their power over others and who define their own
masculinity over and against men they see as in some way abnormal. If, as
one critic argues, the "ability of the narrator to manipulate the discourses
[of stigmatization] . . . affords [him] some sense of agency,"[10] it is an agency
that imitates, self-destructively, the power dynamics of a homophobic and
misogynist male sexuality he sees all around him.

Perhaps the key to understanding *A Boy's Own Story*, then, is this: White
examines his narrator in terms of the normative demands for masculinity
and male power in his culture from which the young man feels excluded,
and he shows how that sense of exclusion warps his narrator's experience in
ways that help explain his betrayal of Beattie. Indeed, that White's purpose
is to explain rather than condemn his narrator is clear if we compare the final
scenes of the novel with its opening one, for there White dramatizes a similar
social dynamic of sexualized male power, except this time it is the narrator
who is victimized. Because these two scenes are separated from each other
by the length of the novel, White gives an impression that his narrator has
grown out of childhood innocence toward adult experience. But *A Boy's Own
Story* is not structured chronologically, so its opening chapter actually takes
place only a few months before the narrator's betrayal of Beattie, when the
narrator is fifteen. The development of the novel does not represent a growth
into experience so much as an indictment of a society whose corruptions
affect even childhood and adolescence.

The opening chapter of *A Boy's Own Story* evokes a pastoral landscape
of life in the woods, where boys fish with their fathers and take romantic
boat rides across moonlit lakes. When a business associate of the narrator's
father comes to stay with the family in their lakeside cabin, bringing his two
sons, Kevin and Peter, it is not long before the older boy, Kevin, finds his way
into the narrator's bed late at night. This adolescent sexual liaison, initiated
by a boy who for all we know does not think of himself as homosexual or

gay, leads the narrator to fantasize about love in the most romantic terms. The scene might be read as White's attempt to communicate to his American readers something many of them didn't seem to know already, even in the 1980s when the novel was published: gay people and adolescents feel love in the same romantic ways others do, and their longing for sexual companionship is a valid expression of that love. But the idyllic structure on which White builds these romantic ideals collapses in an instant, when the narrator chastises Kevin and Peter for horsing around in the boat from which they all have been fishing. "When I asked them to sit still, they gave each other that same smirk and started mocking me, repeating my words, their voices sliding up and down the scale, 'You *could* be more considerate.'. . . Somehow—but at what precise moment?—I had shown I was a sissy. . . . I'd betrayed myself" (30).

Violating a complex and subtle system of social codes that regulate appropriate 1950s masculinity, the narrator reveals himself to be somehow different from Kevin or Peter, not a boy in the ways they are—at least in their eyes. Even though the narrator is older and more experienced, he doesn't know how to resist the boys' implication that he is somehow inferior to them. Unlike the narrator, Kevin has already acquired the power and confidence, at age fourteen, to distance himself from the same-sex desires he feels in himself by stigmatizing them in others. Perhaps Kevin is different from the narrator in the sense that same-sex sex acts seem to represent for him only a momentary pleasure and do not reflect the same persistent desires entangled with romantic longings that the narrator feels. Nevertheless White makes us acutely aware that Kevin exists within different structures of social power and support. As his bonding with his brother suggests, he has a different relationship to men and boys from the narrator. He is confident among males, and he is able to support his understanding of himself in terms other men and boys find mutually empowering.

And because *sissy* is a term that in 1950s America stigmatized both a boy's gender and sexuality, the narrator accepts at face value its implied way of dividing his male gender from his sexuality. So, he reads his desire for Kevin as evidence that he is not really a man at all. In fact, he seems already to have judged himself in these terms, for he says that he "betrays" himself to Kevin and Peter. It is the first and not the only time in the two novels that the narrator is made to see his own feelings for men as denoting a peculiar lack of power that other men take for granted as an aspect of their fully masculine, sexual identities. Understanding the social power dynamics of the opening scene helps us, then, to see more precisely how and why the narrator's betrayal of his teacher a few months later, at the end of the novel, represents his attempt to assume some of these very powers of adult masculinity that he feels he lacks.

But the issue in the novel is not simply one of gender. It is the narrator's specifically gay desire that, ultimately, separates him from the other men and boys he knows. In one particularly moving sequence of events the narrator describes his friendship with Tom, a heterosexual boy who seems willing to overlook the rumors of his unusual sexual activities so long as he (the narrator) understands that Tom doesn't "go in for that weird stuff" (117). Although Tom is a decent fellow and true friend, the situation is similar to the one the narrator finds himself in with Kevin, for both boys draw a line between themselves and the narrator despite their genuine emotional investment in him. Again, the narrator seems to accept such boys' privileged view of things. He says that he understands his "homosexuality [is] a sickness" (118), and, worse, he sees that by dissociating himself from the "weird stuff" Tom is attempting to cleanse himself by locating illness in the narrator: "The medical smell, that Lysol smell of homosexuality, was staining the air again as the rubber-wheeled metal cart of drugs and disinfectant rolled silently by" (117–18).

White makes clear that there simply is no available social script for the narrator to protest Tom's labeling his homosexuality as weird (as mild as that word is in the scheme of things), and none for valorizing the overlapping feelings of desire and friendship he feels for Tom. The irony is that both Kevin's and Tom's emotions are less rich than the narrator's; both are less able to trade in the ambiguities of friendship and desire than he is. Nevertheless, throughout *A Boy's Own Story* White anticipates the groundbreaking analysis of Eve Kosofsky Sedgwick, who critiqued a cultural dynamic in which heterosexual men attempt to disavow their own "homosocial" desires for other men by designating and abjecting a special category, homosexuals, whose marked same-sex desire they wrongly presume to be wholly different from anything they experience themselves.[11]

Indeed, the boundary demarcating the experience of some men from others is powerfully demonstrated in White's novel. The narrator most fears that his homosexuality will cause him to be excluded from the world of men he most desires. "I was becoming frightened," he says. "I was being pushed out of the tribe" of normal, respectable men (164). His erotic and affectional yearning for men is a nearly religious fascination he fears he will be taken from him if it is revealed that he is homosexual, for despite evidence from his own experience, his image of homosexuality is as stereotypical and demeaning as any his society produces:

I was possessed with a yearning for the company of men, for their look, touch and smell, and nothing transfixed me more than the sight of a man shaving and dressing, sumptuous rites. It was men, not women, who struck me as foreign and desirable and I disguised myself as a child or a man or whatever was necessary in order to enter their hushed, hieratic company, my disguise so perfect I never stopped to question my identity. Nor did I want to study the face beneath my mask, lest it turn out to have the pursed lips, dead pallor and shaped eyebrows by which one can always recognize the Homosexual. (169–70)

The narrator longs to live among men, to be like them, and be loved by them. But homosexuality is persistently imaged in 1950s America as not being part of the legitimate world of men. It is little wonder that by the end of the novel he exercises the exclusionary power to symbolically reject his own homosexuality and embrace becoming an adult man by betraying Beattie, whose own social non-conformity stands in symbolically for society's and the narrator's hatred of homosexuality.

A Boy's Own Story raises perhaps the most important question that any "gay novel" could ask: what exactly is the difference between a gay and a straight boy or man, especially when both seem to engage in similar affections? The answer seems to be power, a kind of masculine power to exclude and objectify others, especially those who lack the ability to exercise privileged and exclusionary codes of masculinity. The novel anatomizes and critiques those strategies of adult sexual power the author views as predominant in 1950s, white America, and it explores how they distort its narrator's experience of his sexuality. Although some critics have faulted White for not recognizing his narrator's privilege as a middle-class white male, he criticizes the abuses of such privilege along with his young narrator's desire in wanting to claim them for himself.[12] White's point seems to be that the young man's sexuality necessarily divorces him from the dubious benefits of heterosexuality and gender that straight white middle-class men take for granted in American society. If that divorce justifies the narrator's later search for new and creative ways for understanding his homosexual difference, which the trilogy as a whole records, neither here nor in the next novel of White's trilogy has he reached such a point of understanding.

To be sure, no single truth about sexuality explains White's narrator. He is not simply a sensitive boy whose hopes for love are crushed by a cruel, homophobic society; and he is not merely a boy whose sense of powerlessness and unhappiness causes him to lash out at others he perceives to be socially outcast, like himself. The brilliance of White's novel is that it reveals its narrator as something of both and helps us understand how these contradictions coexist in one person. In fact, White structures his novel to emphasize them. After the opening scene, the novel moves back in time toward its narrator's earliest boyhood memories, and then gradually brings the reader up to date as the novel proceeds. The narrator, we learn, is a gifted and socially isolated boy whose struggle to find friends and companions is familiar to many American adolescents. He is interested in art, and it is partially through artistic images that he discovers and is able to begin giving more positive shape to the inchoate desires he feels for other men.

He is also a precocious sexual adventurer who has had sex and even hired a hustler by the time he meets Kevin at age fifteen. Both his observations and his experience, however, have led him to understand sex as an exercise used by adults to secure power and freedom from social convention, and he has become something of a deceitful manipulator himself as he learns to hide his sexual feelings even as he struggles to enact them. He is not necessarily a likeable young man. But no matter how multiple his facets of person and personality, White makes clear that his adolescence is challenged by society's seemingly monolithic and entirely uncomprehending conviction that homosexuality is a sickness and hence provides him neither freedom nor beneficial power.

If *A Boy's Own Story* reveals society's complicity in creating a narrator whose sense of masculinity and personal power is at odds with his desire for male affection and companionship, the second novel of White's trilogy focuses more fully on the narrator's self-destructive behavior within a larger American world in which he feels alien. *The Beautiful Room Is Empty* covers events in the narrator's life from his last years in high school through college and on to the beginning of his professional career in New York. It ends with his witnessing the uprising at the Stonewall Inn on 27 June 1969, an event that has been represented as the beginning of the modern struggle for gay and lesbian rights, a symbolic turning point in gay life in America. Whether or not the actual historical event can be made to bear such a large burden of significance, the riots function for White as a symbol of both the problem and solution to gay men's self-hatred and inability to find love. As we have already seen, the narrator of *The Farewell Symphony* writes that "the Stonewall uprising changed . . . [gay men's] self-esteem, on which mutual love depends" (29), so it makes sense that in this pivotal moment the narrator of *The Beautiful Room* begins to imagine "foolishly . . . that gays might someday constitute a community rather than a diagnosis."[13] In this respect, *The Beautiful Room Is Empty* acts as a bridge between the narrator's intensely private suffering in the first novel of the trilogy and his feeling of belonging to a community in *The Farewell Symphony*.

Nevertheless, in most ways the narrator of *The Beautiful Room Is Empty* seems more unhappy than ever. Rather than representing him as developing smoothly from childhood unhappiness through adolescent friendships to a mature sense of belonging in a community, the novel continues to represent its narrator—as *A Boy's Own Story* did—as fundamentally divided within a social world that cannot conceive his homosexuality as a mature, fulfilling possibility. Whereas the title of *A Boy's Own Story* suggests that the boy at least has a story to tell, one that ironically recasts and critiques the "salubrious, little-manly world" represented in the Victorian periodical *Boy's Own Magazine*,[14] the title of *The Beautiful Room Is Empty* is taken from a letter written by Franz Kafka to a woman he thought he loved but whose relationship to him was primarily epistolary. The letter evokes the tragic emptiness of two people kept apart through to their inability to inhabit the same place at the same time. It thus describes a sense of isolation and missed opportunity that applies to White's narrator so long as he is unable to move beyond a disquieting sense of discomfort with his own homosexuality.

It is this discomfort that provides the primary thematic substance of White's novel. *The Beautiful Room Is Empty* painstakingly analyzes what the narrator calls his "self-hatred" (74). Not strictly speaking a psychological term or condition, the notion of self-hatred refers to the ways some minority individuals internalize society's negative perceptions and act out behaviors that seem to confirm their damaging validity. While, as we will see, White finds a number of ways to demonstrate how self-hatred affects the lives of his gay characters, perhaps no single demonstration is more complexly rendered than the narrator's use of the term to evoke the disgust he feels for himself when he engages in anonymous sex in the public toilets at his midwestern university. White's work characteristically "shows how effectively sexual acts reveal the psychological nuances of character."[15] White believes that sex is one, if not the, significant difference between gay and straight people, and his novels do not defer to a reader's possible desire to be comforted by ignoring the difference sex makes in the lives of his characters. So, although these scenes are not the novel's first references to gay sex, their description of what may be for many readers the novel's most alienating representation of gay life helps us see something about the complexity of the psychological and social problems that beset its narrator.

White makes the significant point that in the 1950s and early 1960s there were few, if any, respectable outlets in American life for the expression of

gay men's romantic and sexual longings. To be clear, White is no apologist
for respectable, bourgeois sexuality. He does not subscribe to conventional
moral bromides about the inferiority of anonymous public sex to the kinds
most Americans confess to enjoying only in the privacy of their bedrooms. In
fact, later in the novel the narrator will celebrate a type of outlaw sexuality
that binds him in secrecy with other gay men having sex in public toilets in
New York City, even though those scenes too may need to be read in relation
to the early shame the narrator feels about these acts. But here, describing his
narrator's sexual life in the context of a physical need that has few opportunities for expression, White highlights the disgust the narrator feels for
himself and other gay men. Sex, ironically, isolates rather than connects the
narrator to other men like himself. In a telling metaphor, the narrator says
that the toilets are a "harsh exchange where I was selling myself for free but
still could never find enough takers, where the buyers I despised despised the
merchandise I'd become" (84).

Thus the scenes describe an emotional bind at the heart of the narrator's
desire. Living in a world in which there are few outlets for gay men to meet
and socialize, public sex is one of his only options. But the narrator considers
the men he meets there, people like himself, to be damaged goods. Worse,
White uses these scenes to suggest that his narrator fears he is becoming the
figure of the homosexual imagined by society: life-denying and predatory.
The homosexual men the narrator meets are not looking to meet each other.
Rather, "the thrill came when one bagged not another old fruit but a hot
young college kid, for although I myself was at least young and in college, I
already saw myself as vampire-cold, turned prematurely old as a punishment
for vice . . ." (75). Whether one considers the bathroom a symbol for, a cause
of, or simply a location for revealing the narrator's disgust with his sexual
urges, the scenes reveal clearly the ways the narrator feels imprisoned by his
own sexual desires—"There was nothing glamorous about my time in the
toilets, that long sentence I was serving" (74)—and the ways his imprisonment is transforming him, in his own mind, into one of the "john fairies" or
"tearoom nellies," in short, into a "pervert" (66). These scenes show White
at his most merciless in analyzing the damage inflicted on young gay psyches
by society's hypocrisy and disregard—and the effects of such damage are
psychologically diffuse.

When the narrator does find himself in social situations that provide
alternative outlets for his sexual and romantic longing, he seems unable to
embrace them with anything but a masochistic shame similar to what he
experienced in the toilets. Attending a gay dance in a private house with his
friend William Everett Hunton, he is surprised to find a social world outside

the toilets, and he characteristically assumes it is one that he will not be invited to join: "I suspected that handsome gay men all knew each other and avoided public cruising" (102). The line provides additional evidence of the kind of personal devaluation that accompanies the narrator's cruising in the toilets. When, however, he works up the courage to do what no other man at the party will do—ask the most handsome man in the room to dance—he is not only surprised when the man, Harry, says yes, but assumes his dance partner couldn't feel any desire for him, even when Harry kisses him. "He didn't desire me (what god would?)" (104).

Society alone is not to be faulted here, for the narrator makes assumptions about his unworthiness based on a shallow ethic connecting erotic desire to physical beauty. Rather than read the evidence that gay men might be tender and loving with one another, the narrator can only think of himself as foolish for being "a grown man wanting to be sheltered by another" (104). He imagines gay male possibilities as one-time-only encounters. "The freedom to dance with a man . . . ," he continues, "seemed remarkable enough to be a one-time-only privilege, but maybe parties like this one went on all the time. Was there a secret fraternity that linked homosexuals across states, countries, centuries? Was I being rushed?" (104–5). These last sentences point to the irony that by the time White came to write the novel, many homosexual Americans had created communities linking them across states and countries. In fact, the speaking voice of the older narrator appears insistently throughout this scene to point toward all that his younger self missed because he could not see himself and other gay men as worthy of friendship, love, and community.

This protagonist is remarkably changed (and not for the better) from his earlier incarnation in *A Boy's Own Story*. As a fifteen-year-old boy, he was at least able to melt into the comfort of Kevin's love in a way that seems all but closed off to his older self. Here, he takes society's failure to imagine a place for him as evidence that he deserves none. So, he is persistently unable to accept his sexual desire for men as a normal part of his experience. "I hated my sexuality," the narrator says, "and believed it could be redirected" (82). Even more than *A Boy's Own Story*, *The Beautiful Room Is Empty* is replete with the narrator's description of himself and other gay men as sinful and sick. By the end of the novel he echoes, with little irony, the language of a virulently homophobic essay printed in one of the national news magazines when he refers to his homosexuality as a "pathetic malady" (225). Novelist John Rechy rightly sees that the novel explores "the most insidious aspect of oppression, that which causes the oppressed to judge himself, not the oppressor, to annihilate self-esteem, accept shame."[16] Indeed, neither the narrator nor his many friends are able to take gay life and gay people seriously. Although the characters in the novel lead relatively privileged lives as middle-class white men in America, their unhealthy sense of themselves precludes their leading fully healthy, productive gay lives.

Not every gay person takes society's negative evaluation of homosexuality to heart, in the 1950s or today. Nevertheless, because nearly all the gay characters in *The Beautiful Room* do demonstrate disbelief in the validity of their own sexual experience, White clearly emphasizes this peculiar aspect of gay life at the time. The narrator's friend William Hunton, whose entire identity turns out to be a fabrication, decides he is going to go straight, and ends up making one of the narrator's female friends, Annie, more miserable than she otherwise might have been. The narrator's first lover, Lou, rejects bourgeois sexuality and conventional morality at least to the extent that he is willing to "live a life of homosexual crime" (141). It is a romantic gesture, one admired by the narrator, and it echoes the influence in White's work of Jean Genet, who finds his own homosexuality interesting primarily to the extent that it forces him to remain a "complete outsider from the conventional world."[17] But when a new gay magazine appears on the scene (*One* was an actual early gay-interest magazine), Lou is aghast: "Why should a bunch of criminals be allowed to have a *magazine*, for chrissake" (130).

The most tragic instance is Sean, a man the narrator meets and falls in love with towards the end of the novel. He is, the narrator says, "the great love of my life" (216), and the novel briefly holds out hope that the narrator can now imagine how two men might fall in love and be happy when he says that "the idea that [Sean] might like me radically revised my version of who we were" (192). But White recognizes that individual transformations are not possible in a social atmosphere that doesn't support them; *The Beautiful Room Is Empty* is no more a traditional "coming-out novel" than *A Boy's Own Story*. This time, however, it is Sean who "didn't want to be gay." "Waking up beside me," the narrator reports, "was too much evidence for him that he was becoming homosexual" (209). Sean too, it seems, exhibits the kind of self-division in his desires characteristic of the narrator, although in his case it leads toward a psychiatric breakdown, which sends him back to his family in the Midwest. Although we learn in *The Farewell Symphony* that Sean recovers, he and the narrator are never again lovers. White's point is that the social opprobrium against homosexuality shapes its gay characters' responses to themselves and other gay people. They are simply unable to find satisfying relationships with one another—not because they are ill matched but because they devalue their homosexuality, a point White makes when he allows his narrator to talk about a pathfinding earlier gay American novel,

James Baldwin's *Giovanni's Room*. "Giovanni," he says, "stops being attractive the moment he abandons his heterosexuality" (193).

Indeed, so pervasive are his negative attitudes toward his homosexuality that even the narrator's response to the Stonewall Riots is compromised. Although earlier we saw him tentatively imagining that a positive change in gay lives might emerge, his ambivalence expresses itself in "an urge to be responsible and disperse the crowd peacefully, send everyone home. After all," he asks, "what were we protesting? Our right to our 'pathetic malady'?" (225). It is an attitude so sad and self-loathing that White fictionalizes history as a way to explain it. In this version the riot does not even make the morning news: "we couldn't find a single mention in the press of the turning point of our lives" (228). This detail is not historically accurate; the Stonewall Riots were reported in newspapers across America. But White alters history to reinforce the novel's point that society disdains homosexuality, thus confirming the narrator's sense that he and his experiences are not worthy of respect.

"I'm Your Friend": Friendship in *A Boy's Own Story* and *The Beautiful Room Is Empty*

In vivid contrast to these aspects of the novels that explore internal division and self-hatred, White also shows his narrator developing friendships with other gay people that will become fundamental to creating a positive sense of self and strong social communities in his characters' futures. The narrator of *A Boy's Own Story*, who imagines that he is smelly and unlikeable, is obsessed with finding friends. As a gifted child, he has intellectual and artistic longings that put him outside the mainstream of many American boys' interests. Reaching toward adolescence he becomes acutely aware that one great difference between his sister and himself is her seemingly natural capacity to cultivate friends. It is for this reason that his friendship with Tom, when it finally comes about, takes up such a large portion of the first novel in White's trilogy.

The Beautiful Room Is Empty begins on the topic of friendship, and that is where it pretty well ends, too. Its opening chapter focuses on the beginning of the narrator's friendship with Maria, an artist who becomes a lifelong friend and who, more importantly, helps the narrator see that there are people with whom he can share emotional intimacy and camaraderie around his artistic longings. Through his friendship with Maria the narrator begins to find a focused way of understanding himself in relation to and in many ways outside of mainstream American life. Maria gives the narrator a way to understand his artistic longings as legitimate, and she is the first person ever to say to him what many people now take for granted: "being gay . . . isn't such a big deal" (211).

Indeed, White makes clear in *The Beautiful Room Is Empty* that it is primarily through self-affirming relationships with other gay and lesbian people that his narrator discovers the dignity and support necessary to any maturation, sexual or social. In addition to Maria, who confesses that she enjoys sleeping with men but only falls in love with women, the novel portrays the narrator's long-term friendship with Lou, a man who becomes his lover one summer while he is on break from school. This relationship represents something entirely new for the narrator, for throughout both *A Boy's Own Story* and *The Beautiful Room Is Empty,* he is unable to sustain friendly relationships with the men he has slept with. Early in *The Beautiful Room,* the narrator meets a man, Tex, who treats him kindly and with respect. But once the narrator has sex with him, "a wave of sickening guilt" rushes over the narrator and we hear no more about him (46). With Lou the narrator is able to maintain a friendship after they end their sexual relationship, even though the novel records a rather bittersweet conclusion to their story. Lou, like the narrator, is divided about his sexual feelings, and the novel shows the many ways in which he acts out a kind of disdain for them and for himself. These feelings are not unlike those that make the narrator of *A Boy's Own Story* lash out at Beattie, or the narrator of this novel unable to maintain friendships with the people he sleeps with. In Lou's case, they lead him to marry a woman—so he can "settle down" and "make more money" (199).

Not surprisingly, this turn toward bourgeois respectability fails, and Lou comes to repent his actions. As if to highlight the ways such conflicting impulses damage gay men's opportunities for happiness, White shows Lou confessing too late his love for the narrator who has by now fallen in love with Sean. But in this moving moment, it is not the loss of physical love that seems most significant. It is, rather, the revelation of the importance of friendship.

> "And you don't love me anymore?"
> "Lou, you're my best friend."
> "Really?"
> "Yes."
> "I never had a friend. I don't like what's-his-name."
> "Why not?"
> "I'm jealous. You're *my* lover. He's taken you away from me."
> "He hasn't taken me away. I'm your friend. I love you." (208)

Lou's confession occurs in a rare instance of extended direct dialogue in White's early novels, and the simplicity of showing two gay men speak directly to one another with candor about their love and friendship may, in fact, be the emotional climax of *The Beautiful Room Is Empty*, one to which the Stonewall uprising is merely a coda. Indeed, Tony Purvis sees "friendship" in White's works as being greater than any political identification among gay men.[18] So, while Lou and the narrator, being homosexual, may be alienated from society, their relationship as lovers and friends becomes the backdrop against which the narrator will eventually be able to develop a more secure sense of self within the community portrayed in *The Farewell Symphony*.

"A Big Gray Country": Social Dysfunction in *A Boy's Own Story* and *The Beautiful Room Is Empty*

Both *A Boy's Own Story* and *The Beautiful Room Is Empty* analyze the hypocrisies and moral failures of American society and culture, for these, ultimately, betray the country's nonconformists, sexual and otherwise. White reserves special scorn for the psychological professions and their role in reproducing the social opprobrium against homosexuality common in the 1950s. In *A Boy's Own Story*, the narrator seeks treatment for his homosexuality with a psychiatrist, Dr. John Thomas O'Reilly, whose name sardonically references the name a character in D. H. Lawrence's *Lady Chatterley's Lover* gives to his penis. More to the point of White's satire, Dr. O'Reilly relies on Freud's famous talking cure, the idea that patients in psychoanalysis talk themselves into an understanding that leads to cure. Except in this case the doctor does all the talking. O'Reilly "was not a good listener," and "to save time [he] unfolded his ideas at the outset, and then rehearsed them during each subsequent session since, as he explained, although these notions could easily enough penetrate the conscious mind, they soaked less readily into the hairy taproot of the unconscious" (168).

O'Reilly elaborates all the stale clichés about homosexuality commonplace in mid-century psychological thought—the idea that mothers feminize their gay male children, that homosexuality is a symptom of a more profound disturbance, and that it can and must be exchanged for heterosexuality. But neither O'Reilly nor his theories provide evidence that homosexuality is, in fact, an illness. The learned man seems incapable of understanding what even a young graduate student in psychotherapy says to the narrator in *The Beautiful Room Is Empty*: "people don't really change. . . . It's more a question of adjusting, of learning to play the hand you've been dealt" (152). That idea, of course, is the one assumed by most modern psychologists, and in *The Farewell Symphony* we discover the narrator seeking just such therapy.[19]

Both novels represent American middle-class life—ironically from whence proceeds the bulk of the animosity toward homosexuality—as sexually

ravaged and socially dysfunctional. *A Boy's Own Story* reveals the narrator's
father's multiple sexual affairs and harassment of the women who work for
him. It is through his father that the narrator comes to think that one mark of
mature, masculine adulthood is a brutal, competitive power to put other men,
especially ones you don't like, in their place. The work shows as well the finely
tuned filiations of his mother's despair over her inability to find a suitable
partner after her divorce, which perhaps models for the narrator a kind of
sexual abjection that he associates with his desire for men. The novel also
shows adults' willingness to take advantage of the sexual naïveté of the narrator, as when a small-time hustler steals his money by promising to get him
a bus ticket to New York. It presents any number of other adults, themselves
constrained by the homophobic structures of society, who variously tease and
torture the narrator in sexualized situations: Mr. Stone, the camp counselor
who attempts to lure him with "art" photographs of naked young men, or
Mr. Pouchet, the teacher who cultivates the narrator's friendship but lapses
into silence after the young man writes an anonymous love poem to him.

There are kind, well-adjusted adults in *A Boy's Own Story*, people like
Fred and Marilyn who run a bookstore that the narrator frequents and who
become his friends. Both are gay and take the young man seriously, talking
with him respectfully, and acting non-judgmentally when he finally confesses his homosexuality to Marilyn. But, ironically, the impressionable narrator's mother tells him to stop associating with Fred and Marilyn because
she believes they are "Communists and living in sin" (89). Even those
who would seem to be exceptions to the general dysfunctionality of the
sexual world White portrays are constrained by its provinciality and small-
mindedness.

In *The Beautiful Room Is Empty* the narrator speaks about America as a
land of complacent, unthinking people: "It felt, at least to me, like a big gray
country of families on drowsy holiday, all stuffed in one oversized car and
discussing the mileage they were getting and the next restroom stop they'd
be making, a country where no one else was like me—or worse, where there
was no question of talking about the self and its discontent, isolation, self-
hatred, and burning ambition for sex and power" (11). These Americans
are not concerned with ideas. They are rather more identified with their cars
than the larger world around them.

Early in the novel, the narrator's attitude seems to proceed from simple
social snobbery. Insecure with himself, he denigrates others. As the novel
develops, the narrator's critique of America transforms into a fear that the
narrowness of American thought will impede his work as an artist, especially

a gay one. He worries he will have no audience because he has nothing in common with mainstream America: "As a budding writer, I knew I'd never be able to give a convincing account of marriage, birth, parental love, conjugal intimacy, the spicy anguish of adultery—none of the great occasions—until I'd rid myself of this malady which was so narrowing" (148). But it is also in the novel's critique of American complacency that the artist—the gay artist—finds a voice, both intellectual and sexual. After revealing his early fears about the possibilities for his art, the narrator continues:

> And yet something wild and free in me didn't want to give in to them, the big baggy grown-ups. No, if I were perfectly honest (and I couldn't be, I lacked the necessary confidence), I'd have to admit that there was a world run by women and feminized men (not effeminate but feminized men) that I wanted to escape, the world of mild suburban couples, his and her necks equally thick and creased, their white hair similarly cropped. The hard hot penis I grabbed for under the toilet-stall partition or the slow wink of a drag queen looking back at me over her ratty fox neckpiece just before she turned the corner—these glimpses piqued my craving for freedom, despite my yearning after respectability. (149)

American middle-class life is oppressive both in terms of the thought it suppresses and the sex it represses. Speaking in the voice of the older writer looking back on his youthful lack of confidence, the narrator explicitly contrasts a world run by women and feminized men—mild and presumably sexless—with the male-centered, aggressive sexuality he now discovers in the toilets. White has rewritten and complicated the lessons to be learned from public sex. Here it appears as an outlaw strain of sexual revolt from middle-class complacency that, he suggests, may save the narrator from sexual and artistic conformity, revenge perhaps for the lonely imprisonment he felt in his youth. If the tensions of this novel find the narrator endlessly lamenting the "narrowness" of his homosexuality, its critique of American life implies that the narrowness lies elsewhere, in the heartland of a country the narrator will eventually escape.

Ultimately art and homosexuality become locations for creative self-expression and the freedom denied in American life. These are dominant themes White takes up at length in *The Farewell Symphony* and in so doing challenges any simplistic understanding that gay lives can or should be easily assimilated into mainstream American life. In the third novel of his trilogy, gay lives and communities are strongly valued, in and of themselves and in their difference from American norms.

A Whitmanesque World: Sexuality and Art
in *The Farewell Symphony*

As we've seen already, *The Farewell Symphony* can be read as a fulfillment of the "coming-out" narrative deferred in the first two novels of White's trilogy. At the end of *The Beautiful Room Is Empty* and again at the beginning of *The Farewell Symphony,* White references the Stonewall Riots as having marked a symbolic turning point in the lives of gay men in the United States, acknowledging something of a happy or liberated response to the militant homophobia detailed in the earlier two novels. Yet, not surprisingly, *The Farewell Symphony* contextualizes and complicates any simple reading of this change in gay American men's lives, for it is simultaneously a celebration and an elegy that begins in Paris at Père Lachaise Cemetery six months after the death from AIDS of the narrator's lover, Brice, at age thirty-three. Reflecting the structure of *A Boy's Own Story, The Farewell Symphony* then returns to the years just after the Stonewall Riots, more than a decade before HIV appeared among gay men in New York and nearly two decades before the death of Brice.

Moving through the 1970s at a leisurely pace, the novel explores and celebrates the transformation in many gay men's lives that took place in that decade. Ultimately, however, it catches up with the AIDS crisis, recording and memorializing any number of the narrator's dead friends and lovers, and filling in (albeit briefly) the backstory of Brice's death. So, despite the novel's celebration of the achievements of its gay characters over dominant, homophobic discourses in American life, it remains a story about loss and the continuing instabilities of gay life, identity, and community.

The Farewell Symphony is one of White's longest and most complex works, with its delicate balancing of two contrasting stories of gay life. It continues White's sociological narrative by showing his gay characters coming out into a brilliant world of their own making and then transforms that story into an elegy for the passing of that world. By way of its framing device and narrative digressions into the era of AIDS that is always yet to come in the main plot, *The Farewell Symphony* does not let us forget that the rich, emotionally, sexually, and intellectually brilliant world White describes will end. Nevertheless the novel neither denigrates nor second-guesses the validity and worth of that world.

Early in the novel White uses the Stonewall Riots to make a point about gay men and self-love that contrasts his exploration of self-hatred in *The Beautiful Room Is Empty*. Of course, the Stonewall Riots have been seen to mark a false dichotomy in the history of gay life in America, by implying wrongly that all that came before was unhappy or lacking in liberation and that all that came after was progressive or forward looking. Using the Stone-wall Riots to demarcate a totalizing change in gay living also tends to erase the histories of gay and lesbian people outside New York and other big cities who, even in the 1970s, did not have access to the structures for community building available to the middle-class gay men White writes about. For White, however, they stand as a kind of shorthand symbol to mark the difference between gay lives disrupted by self-doubt and those thriving because of newfound self-esteem.

One way to grasp this theme is to consider the contrast in the novel between its narrator's devastating experience of two lost loves, Sean and Brice. White brilliantly sets these two characters in thematic proximity to one another at the beginning and then at the end of the novel, after both have died. If we recall, Sean is the lover from *The Beautiful Room Is Empty* whose inability to accept being gay meant that he could not return the love of the narrator, because it reminded him that he was becoming a homosexual. "He didn't think he was queer," the narrator of *The Farewell Symphony* writes, early in the novel, "and he hated the idea that he might *end up* in the arms of a man" (30). But even though late in the novel the narrator says that Sean is "the person whom I'd loved the most intensely and who awakened in me if not the widest, then the deepest feelings" (412), he also says that Brice is "the first man I'd loved at the same time he loved me" (410). The two lovers' coordinated appearance in the novel thus recalls the differences in the meaning and possibilities of love that have emerged for the narrator over time. They are mirror images of one another that illustrate the importance and value of gay love. As if in response to all the unhappiness and failed relationships of the earlier novels, *The Farewell Symphony* insists on the possibility of love between men, and the enduring bond it creates between individual men and among all the men one has loved.

Most importantly, *The Farewell Symphony* celebrates possibilities for gay friendship, sexual freedom, and community that emerge once the narrator moves beyond the patronizing disdain he had exhibited for gay men in *The Beautiful Room Is Empty*. It is difficult to summarize the novel in this regard, but its long, panoramic structure reveals a dense and interlocking series of friendships and loving relationships of all sorts, and thus brings to fruition the theme of friendship so important to White's trilogy. Within this brave new world of social and sexual difference, the narrator forges profound and life-altering friendships with a number of men, Butler, Max Richards, Eddie, and most significantly, Joshua—to name just a few. The narrator's taking part in this community of friends enables his growth and intellectual development. His friendships are central to the narrator's ability to create himself as a self-respecting gay man even as they allow him to develop as an artist. There is a great and vivid contrast between the two earlier novels, which represent the narrator's aspiring to become a writer, and this one, in which he is revealed to be one (even if he is not yet fully successful). Indeed, because *The Farewell Symphony* resolves some of the tensions around narration that are apparent throughout the trilogy, it seems in some ways to be about its narrator's assuming his voice both as a gay man and an artist.

The first two novels of the trilogy often highlight the complex negotiation between the story they tell and the narrator who tells it. White creates the illusion that it is his younger self telling his "own story" when in fact the novels are narrated by an older version of the boy or adolescent whose story is being told. This narrator is an infinitely wiser, tolerant speaker who understands his adolescent desires better than his young self does, and who thus represents a more enlightened point of view about the sexual and other issues taken up in the works. The presence of at least two narrative voices in White's earlier novels reflects brilliantly two selves made different in the change of social circumstance, two different identities represented in an only seemingly continuous fictional persona.

Through this double narration White is able to create sympathy for characters who do not always behave in ways conducive to their own or others' happiness, for the older narrator proposes reasons why his characters behave as they do. More to the point, the enlightened presence of the older narrator suggests that his younger self will grow into a richer character than he at present seems to be. One critic, Reed Woodhouse, faults White for speaking too assuredly on behalf of his younger protagonists and for failing to leave them to the judgment of the reader. He suggests that White's early autobiographical novels seem more like memoirs than fictions. The "gorgeous prose" of White's older narrator reveals him to be too much like White himself, in love with language and not true to the experience of his young protagonists.[20]

Seen another way, however, the novels' highlighting of a narrative voice much like White's own allows the novelist to foreground the need for his gay characters to invent themselves and assume the voices they have hitherto been denied. White's biographer Stephen Barber points out that White's use of autobiographical materials in *The Farewell Symphony* creates a "sense of total transparency . . . the whole truth of the writer's presence, of the reader's presence, and of the presence of the narrative process itself."[21] In other words, in the final novel of the trilogy White seems to speak for himself directly to the reader about what it means to write his particular story.

Of course, it is worth remembering that none of these narrators actually is White himself, Woodhouse's argument notwithstanding. They are personae carefully constructed to achieve particular emotional and thematic effects. But the narrator of *The Farewell Symphony* assumes a degree of control over the narrative that makes him and this novel different from the earlier ones. He is no longer divided; he no longer needs to be interpreted through an older self who understands better the social processes that bind him. This narrator speaks on his own behalf, and defines the meaning of his own life and experience. And once we hear his voice, we realize that he has been speaking to us all along in the earlier novels.

His voice stands in synecdoche for gay and lesbian people's insistence on their own legitimacy and complexity as human beings, people entitled to speak on their own behalf. Tony Purvis argues that White's novels always reveal that "sexual identities are clearly textual constructions";[22] that is, they demonstrate an understanding that sexual identities are not something that exists prior to the individual. They are not transcendent categories into which individuals are slotted at birth, but products of discourses that shape individuals and that can also be shaped by those individuals. *The Farewell Symphony* is perhaps the best example in White's autobiographical novels of how that is so, for in telling the story of its narrator's life seemingly simultaneously with his living it, the novel foregrounds the very processes of reporting through which it and its characters' identities are revealed to be creative, social constructions.

It is through his shaping discourse, through the writing of the novel itself, that White helps to refashion not only his own but America's sense of the value of gay life, no matter how variously that idea may be interpreted by gay people themselves. The novel makes a powerful claim that something really has changed after Stonewall, that some coming out really has occurred. Gay and lesbian people now have a productive sense of power, agency, and control over the discourses through which their lives are constituted. Indeed, they have created discourses to replace those outdated ones that haunted the narrator of *A Boy's Own Story* in the image of "the Homosexual" (170).

In many respects *The Farewell Symphony* is a philosophical novel engaged in a sustained analysis of the cultural creativity and sexual experimentation that led in the 1970s to the rise of culturally empowered gay communities. The narrator and his friends form a community of thinkers responding to one of the central preoccupations of White's novel: how to reinvent oneself anew when the social parameters for thinking about sexuality change as drastically as they did in 1970s America. Neither here nor elsewhere is White single-minded about what it means to be or become gay.

The novel presents a wide range of ideas on the topic, many of them not flattering. Max Richards, for instance, "said that homosexual couples were plagued by the 'incest taboo'" (146); a famous writer, Ridgeway, objects to what he sees as Jean Genet's "wallowing in his perversion" (189); and the narrator himself is scornful of the ways gay identities in the 1970s were being commodified by dominant culture, so that some gay men, like mainstream Americans of his father's generation, came to identify themselves through the cars they drove. "Can you imagine debating the virtues of a Corvette and an Eldorado convertible for an entire evening?" he asks (293). These ideas contrast nicely with the narrator's gay idealism: "We were intent on dismantling all the old marital values and the worst thing we could be accused of by one of our own was aping the heterosexual model" (246). Never mind that the narrator end ups, after meeting Brice, defending the couple again. *The Farewell Symphony* stages its ideas as debates about what it means to live and how one ought to live as a gay man. And it suggests that there are many different ways to do so.

Nor does White shy away from deconstructing the pretenses to normality that define heterosexuality in Western life. *The Farewell Symphony* not only examines and reveals gay (white and middle-class) sexualities, it interrogates straight ones as well. At one point in the novel, the narrator suggests that heterosexuals who take their relationships to be defining of who they are, and who lack a "self-mocking" capacity to see their own sexual lives as changeable, are incompetent at negotiating romantic disaster (89). The novel criticizes the ways some heterosexuals even in the 1970s and later see gay life as "aberrant" while indulgently viewing their own sexual sins and peccadilloes as a "source of pride" (92). In the "old, established world of man and woman" the narrator says, "sexuality was used as a bright bait, as reward or recompense, in a game that otherwise concerned suitable pairings, the suitability determined by money, age, religion, race" (178). White's novel refuses the presumption of heterosexuality to imagine itself an ideal against which to value others.

One difficulty in understanding all of White's work is the overlap among categories of relationships that conventional sexual moralists arrange separately. White seems to believe that one might feel love, sex, and friendship in varying combinations for any individual. Indeed, his work explores the ways one might feel any or all these emotions—at the same or different times—for any one person or a number of people. The narrator represents this interplay in utopian terms that presage a new and better world. "We saw gay men as a vanguard that society would inevitably follow. I thought that the couple would disappear and be replaced by new, polyvalent molecules of affection or Whitmanesque adhesiveness" (341). New relationships, new forms of sexual connection, and a new understanding that loving one's self means loving other gay men herald the development of new kinds of sexual association both among gay men and other Americans, ones that move beyond the couple and monogamy. Sex, his narrator writes, is "that sticky semen-glue that bound us together" (367).

The novel, thus, reflects the optimism about new understandings of sex that were widespread in the 1970s, an optimism White seems to want to recover in the era after AIDS. Although White is characteristically forthright about sex and its value, none of his other fictions details with such explicitness the varieties of sexual experimentation taking place in 1970s gay New York or makes such large claims for its importance to the construction of gay identity and community. At one point, the narrator refers to what he calls his "code of bodily sincerity" (148) and, in another place, "the simple authenticity of [the] body" (342). Rather than being the location of social and moral opprobrium, the body is an expressive tool of sexual pleasure, and sex itself becomes a meaningful conduit for interpersonal connection, love, and social community: "I'd always explored the unique mystery of each man I held in my arms and during sex I'd never thought about another" (148).

Indeed, in *States of Desire* (1980), which was written during the historical period covered in White's novel, the novelist lamented the fact that sex in Western culture had been made to bear too much social and moral weight. With the decreasing influence of religion in our culture, he wrote, sex itself was transformed into a mode of transcendence, a way to confirm one's personal worth, and demonstrate the validity of love—all moral projects the novelist labels as "absurd." In the future, he predicted, led by gay men, "sex will be restored to its appropriate place as a pleasure, a communication, an appetite, an art; it will no longer pose as a religion, a reason for being."[23] It is precisely such a sexual ethic that White seems to celebrate in *The Farewell Symphony*.

Such celebration of the role and place of sex in gay social life was bound to be controversial, coming as it did in the years following the worst of the AIDS crises in the United States. Even before the novel was published in America and had only just appeared in London, the gay novelist Larry Kramer wrote an essay in *The Advocate,* an American gay and lesbian news magazine, deploring *The Farewell Symphony*'s numerous and explicit representations of gay sex. Kramer suggested that White had failed to show that gay men "brought AIDS upon [themselves] by a way of living that welcomed it."[24] White defended himself by arguing that the role of the novelist is to bear "witness to what [gay men] really [lived] through, not what revisionists and moralists would have preferred."[25] Nevertheless White is not inattentive to the ironies of his celebration of sex in light of AIDS. In fact, both here and in *The Beautiful Room Is Empty*, White several times employs metaphors suggesting that the "sticky semen-glue" that binds gay men together is also the semen that transmits AIDS.

Shortly after the incident in which the narrator of *The Beautiful Room* dances with the man-god, Harry, the narrator—speaking as his older self who is looking back on the events of his youth—intrudes upon the story in one of the few references to AIDS to be found anywhere in that novel: "Anyone who ever let me in his body or arms I still feel grateful to. That's why so many of my friends are old lovers, I suppose. And that includes, these days, dying and dead friends as well, to whom the flesh, my flesh, still connects me" (105). The passage suggests that sex creates a physical connection between men, one that includes connection with the "dying and dead," so that it necessarily reminds us that HIV also connects gay men to one another through their bodily contacts. In *The Farewell Symphony*, one can hardly hear the narrator's defense of his many sexual contacts, and his reference to the traditional couple's disappearance to be replaced by "new, polyvalent molecules of affection," without at least pausing to think about those other molecules, viral ones, that were threatening to effect the disappearance not of a social convention but living and breathing human beings (341).

But there are also molecules of affection and identification that aren't viral—as we've seen, friendship, love, community, and even philosophy count for something. So, rather than view AIDS as a moral effect of promiscuous sexual activity, as Kramer does, White teases out a different understanding of sex and its connection to the disease, one in which AIDS tragically undermines new possibilities for thinking about sexual ethics emerging everywhere around his gay characters. In other words, White laments the way AIDS alters the very "Whitmanesque" possibilities his novel celebrates. Framed as it is by an AIDS narrative, and ending as it does with the narrator's reporting the deaths of many friends and acquaintances, the story of gay love, community achievement, and self-narration in *The Farewell Symphony* is tenuous indeed. AIDS threatens to take back everything that has been gained. Three brief examples will suffice to make the point.

First, if Brice is a replay of Sean in a more productive key, he is nevertheless lost to the narrator just as Sean had been. Second, during the course of the novel, the narrator gives an account of one of his lovers, Leonard, who grew up "in Florida in a trailer camp," with a father who called him a "creep" every time he saw him (324). Leonard moves to New York, where he remakes himself completely. His accomplishments are large and his cultural knowledge profound, so that he no longer sees himself as a "creep" but part of a vibrant, complex community. But when his body succumbs to AIDS, he becomes "once again the despised creep he'd been as a boy" (381). Most telling, the narrator, whose voice had seemed poised to legitimate gay living, is rendered silent by the death of Brice. The reporter of this brave new gay world stumbles into pained silence when, in the final pages of the novel, he tries to tell us what happened to Brice in the moments before his death in Morocco: "I can't go on. I can't tell this story, neither its happy beginning nor its tragic end" (411).

White understands AIDS as destabilizing the possibilities for gay love, esteem, and community in some of the same ways that dominant homophobia had in the years when the narrator was growing up. The irony of AIDS is that it "seemed all of a piece with the hate promulgated by know-nothing American fundamentalists" (364). The disease calls into question the notion of change and transformation in gay life, which is shown to rely not simply on individual will but social and natural circumstance. In response, the narrator's voice undergoes a subtle transformation. If the narrator had imagined himself giving living voice to gay lives in ways they had not, so far, been voiced in American life, he ends up memorializing those lives instead. The novel, the narrator's words, becomes a monument to those lost to AIDS: "I wanted to build a monument of words for Joshua, big and solid, something that would last a century, although I doubted I had the ability" (409). Joshua's spirit, he writes, is "lodged" in his pages, at least he hopes (413). If the narrator's tenuousness, his modesty, nods toward a traditional understanding that words alone cannot capture the spirit of a living human being, he recognizes as well that Joshua and others like him cannot be lost to history if he records their lives in words. In this respect, the novel holds forth possibilities for a future beyond AIDS that its characters perhaps cannot yet imagine.

What White captures in the closing pages of *The Farewell Symphony* is something that has been implicit in its argument throughout: the dependence of gay life on invention, creative response to the challenges of life, and perpetual self-creation. Indeed, one implication of the work is that AIDS may transform the terms of that reinvention but not undo the process, for which the novel itself stands as metaphor. In this respect, the novel is anything but a traditional coming-out story. It is not a tale about one individual's happiness but a script that recalls to the memory of future readers what has been lost and gained. The title of the novel references a Haydn symphony in which the orchestra slowly leaves the stage until only two violins remain to complete the work. Although White seems to get the fact of Haydn's symphony wrong, suggesting that only one violin remains, his point may be to emphasize the narrator's ultimate loneliness. But the novel, like the symphony, is a work of art that can be endlessly replayed in history so that its characters and the people they represent are never lost. It stands as a model for the creative re-inscription of experience that moved gay men beyond self-hatred and that opens new paths for them after and beyond AIDS.

CHAPTER THREE

AIDS Fiction

The Darker Proof, Skinned Alive, and *The Married Man*

Even if *A Boy's Own Story, The Beautiful Room Is Empty,* and *The Farewell Symphony* convey something of a coherent life story, White develops in each a specific narrative strategy to bring his themes and perspectives into focus. A similar virtuoso concern with narrative technique marks the short stories he began to write in the 1980s—collected in *The Darker Proof: Stories from a Crisis* (1987) and *Skinned Alive* (1995)—as well as the follow-up novel to his trilogy, *The Married Man* (2000). These works form a tenuous grouping united not by form or chronology but their emphasis on a theme that has been important to White all along, the place of sex and the body in gay men's lives. Many of them revisit the theme in light of the AIDS crisis in the 1980s, which devastated individuals and threatened the communities of gay men that had been developing steadily over White's lifetime. Some of the stories also take up issues of aging that were of increasing concern to White as he approached his sixties and that would dominate a later collection of stories, *Chaos* (2007). The body, then, is a starting point for White's critical analysis of individuals within larger cultural frameworks in gay American life that were being altered by two factors White (himself HIV positive) understood intimately: the threat of disease and the decay of age.

The Darker Proof

White co-authored *The Darker Proof: Stories from a Crisis* with the British writer Adam Mars-Jones, contributing two stories to the original British edition: "An Oracle," which had already been published in the gay magazine *Christopher Street* in 1986, and a story written specifically for the collaboration, "Palace Days." In the subsequent American edition (published in 1988), he added a third story, "Running on Empty." All three would later be reprinted (some slightly revised) in *Skinned Alive,* but the context of their original publication lends them special urgency because White and Mars-Jones were among the first writers to begin fashioning a literary response to AIDS.

Characteristically, White was already highly evolved in his thinking about how to represent the disease in writing. He and Mars-Jones chose the short story, White has said, as a way of avoiding the "inevitable trajectory" of the novel in which "you begin healthy and end sick and dead."[1] So, even in making the choice to write stories rather than novels, White resisted what, at the time, would have been a dominant association of AIDS with sickness and death. Like many of White's other fictions, these stories reject an over-all narrative explaining the characters and their lives in terms of growth, development, and acceptance or resolution, thereby revising the easy assurances about the meaningful nature of a life such narratives promise. Instead, as Peter Christensen argues, the form of the stories in *The Darker Proof* emphasizes individual moments in the lives of characters who themselves have lived primarily "'for the moment' without much thought of the future." And they end in epiphany, at a moment in which their protagonists achieve a new awareness about the possibilities for living.[2] The epiphanic ending, the moment of insight around even a trivial event, encourages readers to think about what might constitute an appropriate response to the characters' situations rather than simply assume they know already that the story will end tragically. It is a brilliant strategy that emphasizes the possibilities of life even under the threat of death.

These stories are united in their assumption that AIDS was not in any simple way "caused" by gay men or their behavior. The disease is represented rather as one of the unfortunate things that happen to people, and those who get it are no more culpable than people whose bodies grow old and wither. "It's not a reward for promiscuity," one of the characters in the short story "Palace Days" says. "It's just bad luck" (165). Nowhere is White's literary craftsmanship more assured or his vision more broad and humane than in these stories that discover new ways to understand AIDS, gay bodies, and gay sex without succumbing to mythologies of guilt or narratives of homosexuality as disease. Such thinking, White seems to suggest, would take gay people back to square one, the days in which their homosexuality was considered a pathology to be cured, a shameful disorder to be hidden from view.

The three stories in *The Darker Proof* focus on what John M. Clum identifies as a "major theme of gay AIDS literature . . . what to do with a lost past, which was both affluent and carefree," even as they "resist self-hating expla-nations of AIDS."[3] All three explore the tension around a present in which characters attempt to understand their illnesses and their past lives, which were more carefree. Significantly the pasts evoked are remarkably dissimilar, pointing toward the variety of lives that are disrupted by AIDS rather than a simple identification of the disease with undifferentiated gay promiscuity. This distinction is important, and not only because Larry Kramer had sug-gested even as early as 1981—when the *New York Times* report of a "Rare Cancer Seen in 41 Homosexuals" presaged the future crisis—that "many things we've done over the past years may be all that it takes for a cancer to grow from a tiny something-or-other that got in there who knows when from doing who knows what."[4] The critique Kramer was making within gay com-munities—one that reflected, as Bergman points out, many of Kramer's own troubling ideas about gay life, bourgeois respectability, and sexuality[5]—was also being employed by people outside those communities to denigrate gay people by once again associating them with disease and death. As political commentator and erstwhile presidential candidate Patrick Buchanan put it at the time, homosexual men "have killed themselves because they could not or would not control their suicidal appetites."[6]

But as Les Brookes notes, "there is no surrender" to dominant cultural attitudes about AIDS and death in White's stories. "Gay identity is reasserted in a context in which AIDS itself figures as an oracular utterance offering possibilities of renewal to gay men through new modes of intimacy and soci-ality."[7] In her early analysis of AIDS, Susan Sontag pointed out that in the 1970s people had been assured by medicine that "the easy curability of sexu-ally transmitted diseases (as of almost all infectious diseases) made it possible to regard sex as an adventure without consequences."[8] If gay men, who were in the vanguard of the sexual revolution and had acted on these assurances, were not responsible for having formulated them, they were nevertheless to suffer some of the worst consequences to arise from such sureties. So, to accuse them of bringing it on themselves could only have worsened their pain without creating a solution for it—and thus, in itself, become an unethical response to the disease. Without retreating on his essential insight into and celebration of the new possibilities for positive modes of gay being that sex provided in the 1970s, White attempts to understand how AIDS leads to a necessary re-consideration of those possibilities—a theme he had only begun to explore in *The Farewell Symphony*.

"Running on Empty," for instance, tells of Luke's return to the United States after having lived in France for several years. The eighth of ten chil-dren born to his Texan father and Chicana mother, Luke had been a "brilliant student" who had "done everything expected of him."⁹ But, not surprisingly, Texas and his "miserable, mocking family" offer little promise for Luke, so he secures a job in a "Jewish private school just outside New York" (214), where he succeeds brilliantly. Subsequently he becomes a translator and moves to Paris. Luke does not pursue a conventional gay life either in New York or Paris, but seeks instead "sex with workingmen, straight men or close approximations of that ideal" (216). Like many young men from rural America, Luke doesn't identify with gay ghetto communities in places like New York, and, in fact, he doesn't even consider himself gay. So he is surprised to find himself ill with a disease that he—like many Americans at the time the story was written—associates primarily with gay men. Despite White's revelation of such ironies in Luke's self-conception, the thrust of the story concerns his visit to relatives in Texas, especially his interaction with his favorite cousin, Beth, who has dutifully stayed home to begin her own family among her relatives.

The story's tensions develop around the two cousins' differing decisions about how they have pursued their lives, tensions wrapped up with Luke's illness and that come to a head when Beth and Luke encounter a group of drunken teenage boys horsing around, with one urinating off the bed of their pick-up truck. Whereas their carefree lives provoke desire and remembrance in Luke, their actions anger Beth, who seems to see in them a type of irre-sponsibility similar to that which she thinks led to Luke's becoming ill. Luke is "offended that a virus had been permitted to win an argument. He'd been the one to learn, to leave home, to break free. He'd cast aside all the old sins, lived freely—but soon Beth could imagine he was having to pay for his follies with his life" (230–31). In this moment, whose meanings and emotions are revealed in the most muted of ways, White contrasts the self-righteous judg-ment it is possible to make about AIDS with Luke's defense of himself for taking the gamble to live in his own way, free of his family and the narrow obligations they created for him.

In this story about moving away from home and transatlantic crossings, the question of whether Luke is running toward or from something—or both—makes it difficult to know exactly how to place AIDS in the equation of his life. Would he have had a sexual or romantic life if he had stayed in Texas? Would he have avoided illness? Would such a trade-off have been worth it? Beth's husband is already dead of an early heart attack, so White makes clear there are no guarantees in life. By posing the questions of Luke's life in just these ways White avoids the easy answers about AIDS that were emerging in public discussions in the United States in the 1980s. That avoid-ance seems to be one of the points of this complicated story, that and White's insistence on the need to live fully—for although Luke's tank has run dry, he is, to his credit, still running. In the closing moments of the story, Luke returns to the place where the boy had urinated and looks for "traces of that stain under the tree" (233). In a gesture White describes as a "ceremony of doing something actual," Luke finds the spot and touches the dirt to his lips (233). It is a small act of identification with and desire for the young, living boys, but in it Luke finds new life: "He started running again, chewing the grit as though it might help him to recuperate his past if not his health" (233).

The need to get on with living is a theme White works out as well in "An Oracle," one of his most celebrated stories. When Ray's lover George dies, Ray goes "through a long period of uncertainty" (168) during which "he scarcely knew how or why to pick up the threads" of his life (172). Unable to grieve properly and unable to resume his life because of fear and uncertainty brought on both by his life with George and the new possibilities of the disease, Ray experiences AIDS as a threat to his very self. As Richard Dellamora points out, White thereby recognizes and responds to "the solvent effect" of AIDS on "earlier ideas of gay identity."[10] But if the details about Ray's relationship and his efforts in nursing his lover through his final illness make George seem self-centered, manipulative, and controlling, George, it turns out, points the way toward Ray's transformation and new life.

When Ray goes to Crete to escape the grim reminders of death all around him in New York, he meets a young man, Marco. Although their sexual relationship is at first economic, they fall in love with one another, and Ray indulges a fantasy of moving to Crete to live with Marco. But his fantasy accords neither with the realities of Marco's life in a small, family-centered town nor his own realities as an American confronting AIDS. Marco tells Ray that he has to go home and resume his life in words that almost exactly reflect those George had said to him repeatedly during his final illness: "You must look out for yourself" (209). His words are oracular in that they channel George's concern for Ray through Marco's love. They provide another type of epiphany that allows Ray to begin to grieve in earnest and look toward a future that doesn't have to be put on hold. "An Oracle," then, is a story about the persistence of love through the AIDS crisis, but it is also about the need to continue working to "enable a sense of self among male lovers" that is under threat from AIDS.[11]

"Palace Days" is perhaps the most complex of the three stories in *The Darker Proof,* partly because it evokes the ways the past exerts continuous pressure on the present. HIV becomes the primary symbol of the weight of the past. No matter how hard they try, the story's main characters Ned and

Mark simply cannot escape AIDS and their past lives. Formerly Mark had made a successful living as a gay travel agent in New York, until "things fell apart in 81" and his business began to suffer as a result of the voluminous misinformation circulating about AIDS in the early 1980s (132). Relocating to Paris, Mark and Ned "hoped the party would go on in Europe as it had before in the States" (137). But the fact that it does not is constantly borne in on Mark by the gradual failure of his business. While both Ned and Mark have relationships outside their own sexless partnership, "Palace Days" focuses on Mark's relationship with Hajo, a film producer he meets in Venice. As Hajo, like the rest of Europe, becomes increasingly concerned about the HIV that had at first seemed confined largely to North America, he insists that he and Mark get tested. As things go, Mark turns out to be positive and Hajo negative. That difference comes increasingly between them until Mark decides it is better for them to be friends, leaving him at the end of the story with only Ned to face the future.

It is in the elaboration of Mark and Hajo's relationship that White makes some of his most powerful statements about AIDS and the burden of the past it represents. Both men seem somewhat shallow in imaging there is a world beyond or outside AIDS. Mark had thought the party could go on indefinitely, and Hajo accuses Mark of not being careful, of being too promiscuous, as if he had deliberately brought his illness on them both. When, late in the story, Hajo tells of two of his own friends who have died, he seems to think of their deaths as the inevitable consequence of their promiscuity. It is a remark that causes Mark to flare up uncharacteristically, but in a way that indicates his deepening understanding of his situation. Referring to the death of his own friend, Joshua, Marks says that "if Joshua had sex ten times in the last five years that would be a lot. It's not a reward for promiscuity, Hajo. It's just bad luck" (165). AIDS is an ever-present part of one's past. It is a dimension of all these characters' lives that pursues them in the present and into the future. But White suggests that one is not in any simple way responsible for one's past, and certainly one cannot revise it from the present. If we think of AIDS as the reward for gay promiscuity, we will not understand what it means that even the non-promiscuous, even those without the past that Hajo attributes to them, died.

On one level, "Palace Days" is about the ways different men negotiated what it meant to love other men in an era when there were no effective treatments for HIV infection. On another, it is about how AIDS was changing—and not for the better—gay men and the communities they created. But the story implies even more. White seems to suggest that AIDS threatens to extinguish not only individuals, but new ways of seeing and understanding life and sex that were emerging in gay thought in the 1970s. This idea emerges most clearly in connection with Mark's brilliant friend Joshua (perhaps the same character we meet in *The Farewell Symphony*). In telling the story of how Mark and Joshua met at the ballet, White indulges what seems on the surface a gratuitous conversation.

The story tells us that Mark loved the ballet because it provided "a foreglimpse of paradise" in its focus on physical prowess (136). But Joshua, characteristically, sees the art form's meaning more profoundly, as a utopian gesture that unites the "physically deformed, argumentative New York intellectuals in the audience" around its "nonverbal and sublimely athletic" "vision of society" (137). White, thus, subtly shifts the grounds upon which New Yorkers gay and straight meet from an exclusively aesthetic and verbal cultural arena to one bounded by the physical and nonverbal. In other words, Joshua interprets the ballet as an allegory in which disparate groups of people are able to commune through physical, nonverbal communication, which, given White's celebration of the body throughout his work, can be interpreted as entirely salutary. Because Joshua is himself dying of AIDS, the story reminds us of the fragility of the physical as well and, more important, of the ways the death of brilliant thinkers like Joshua decimates thought and insight that may have the potential to reshape everyone's lives for the better.

At the end of the story, we learn that Joshua and his ideas are not side notes to the story, but essential to it. Mark attends a ballet in Paris, *Dances at a Gathering* by the American choreographer Jerome Robbins. He is bitterly disappointed in the performance partly because it reminds him of Joshua, but more so because he discovers that these dancers simply cannot comprehend the work's cultural importance for American people and ideas that are now under severe threat. Mark recognizes that the promise of blessing implied by the old hymn on which the ballet is based ("We gather together to ask the Lord's blessing") is irretrievably lost: "Now there was no Lord left to ask anything of" (166). Worse, the faith in art and ideas that Joshua had taught Mark would replace God seems to melt under the banality of the performance in this new context. The moment symbolizes many losses: Joshua and his humane vision of a utopian future, the innocence of the sexual dance performed by gay men in Mark's world, and the comfort of a sense of home that Mark knew "wasn't there anymore" (167). For one critic, the ballet symbolizes "the vanished ideals of the gay movement, betrayed and abandoned in the panic and aftermath of the AIDS crisis."[12] "Palace Days" provides White's bleakest commentary on AIDS, for unlike the end of *The Farewell Symphony* in which art persists as memory and memorial of what is lost, it is not clear here that even art and ideas will survive the physical loss from disease and death. One's history cannot be blamed for AIDS, but AIDS, it seems, is to blame for the potential end of gay history.

The one glimmer of hope comes in the final sentences of the story, when Mark realizes that Ned is the "only home" he has (167). But such an ending may or may not be positive. It may signify catharsis leading to a renewed appreciation of Ned; or it may point toward Ned's inability to make up for all that is lost. It seems clear, however, that Ned represents a past that Mark cannot escape, so the moment recalls the tensions of the story as a whole.

Skinned Alive

Skinned Alive is the title of a collection that includes the three stories published in *The Darker Proof* as well as five additional tales. In the subsequent paperback edition, White added a sixth. The new works were written and some were published individually during the years in which White was completing work on his biography of the French playwright and novelist Jean Genet, which explains what only seems like White's falling away from the prolific fictional output of his early career.[13] The stories in *Skinned Alive* are not all about AIDS, and those that are handle the disease somewhat tangentially, primarily in reference to the sero-positive status of narrators who are nevertheless recalling stories of happier times. But, in this, as in their emphasis on a sex-positive ethic, youthful desire, and friendship, they help contextualize the stories from *The Darker Proof* as well as the disease itself, so the collection has its own integrity.

Many of the stories in *Skinned Alive* recall the past that threatens to be lost in the absence of some creative response to AIDS, one of which, of course, is the writing of stories. "Reprise," "Cinnamon Skin," and "Watermarked" are told by an autobiographical narrator reminiscent of White himself, one much like the narrators in White's autobiographical novels. Because they recall the past from the vantage point of a present in which AIDS has shaped their experience, the narrators seem to corroborate the pleasures and the loves of their pasts as lasting rebukes to the disease and its effects. "Pyrography," the opening story of the collection, echoes and elaborates a time and events that seem to belong to the era of *A Boy's Own Story*. As such, it testifies to the enduring knowledge of sexuality in White's experiences that are not gainsaid by disease and death. Finally, in "Skinned Alive" and "His Biographer," White reflects on writing and art, so that they, too, stand in testimony against the bleak pessimism of the other stories.

Notwithstanding Peter Christensen's argument that it is only in the AIDS stories that White employs an epiphanic structure, many of the stories in *Skinned Alive* conclude with a moment of re-signification. Their endings invite the reader to imagine anew the meanings of the characters' lives, as if they demanded interpretation in relation to a significant fragment of experience that does not conclude the stories in a traditional sense. The endings do not provide closure so much as they invite the reader to speculate on the multiple significances of the narrative to which they are, often seemingly oddly, appended. In this, the stories suggest that life itself unfolds in ways not easily known or knowable, so that they mark a return to some of the techniques of postmodern fiction White explored in his earliest novels.

A notable example, "Cinnamon Skin," first appeared in *The New Yorker*, and was later reprinted in *Boys Like Us: Gay Writers Tell Their Coming Out Stories*, before being added to the paperback edition of *Skinned Alive*. Although it begins with its narrator's announcement that he is going to tell of "one of God's miracles [that] occurred when [he] was thirteen," it is in some ways a very bleak tale.[14] "Cinnamon Skin" returns to 1953 to recall its narrator's presumably first sexual encounter, with a pianist in a bar in Acapulco while on vacation with his father and stepmother. As in *A Boy's Own Story*, White does not shy away from portraying adolescent desire, and here he ups the ante by making this a story of cross-generational sex. The story records the narrator's disappointments with his lover's businesslike performance, but by any account it seems also a triumphal expression of adolescent desire, confidence, and sexual ingenuity.

Nevertheless it ends with a brief coda describing the narrator's return to Mexico City as an adult, where he finds not the romantic landscape of his memory but a "dirty and crumbling" city whose misfortune seems to reflect his own despair at being sero-positive (273). The story thus movingly evokes a feeling for the way time, AIDS, and aging create a vivid contrast between a past in which one might look with hope toward the future and a present overwhelmed with death. Perhaps no moment anywhere in White's work expresses as cogently the author's refusal to make a causal connection between past sex and AIDS as the gap in time and chronology that separates the triumphant coming-out story from the mournful coda of "Cinnamon Skin." And no other moment expresses so poignantly the despair that is left inarticulate in that silence.

Looked at one way, "Reprise" fills in this gap. Here the narrator recounts the story of an affair he had with Jim Grady when he was fourteen, the discovery of which led to his being sent to an all-male boarding school and a psychotherapist. (It is a different version of White's narrator's story of coming out in *A Boy's Own Story*, and so reminds us that, while both works are based on White's life, the facts are fictionalized for the purpose of each work and White's narrators are not necessarily the same character from story to story.) The primary movement of "Reprise" emerges in response to Grady's re-appearance in the narrator's life forty years later, after the narrator has been diagnosed HIV positive.

The story, thus, says something about the persistence of desire and affection in spite of all. Once again Grady has sex with the narrator, as seemingly unconcerned now with the narrator's disease as he had been when in his youth he did not let the narrator's mononucleosis dissuade him from passion. The narrator wonders if their lives might have been "a bit less deformed" if they had stayed together as a couple, so that the story raises the question of how a different past may have led to a different future (172). But it doesn't focus on the "what ifs" so much as celebrate the ways that AIDS and aging do not, in themselves, preclude reconnecting with what is valuable in the past or with love itself. The story gives vivid expression to White's faith in the body as a conduit of love and desire that crosses physical and temporal boundaries.

"Watermarked" also returns to past events, this time in a way the helps explain how and why gay men developed the sexual lives they did. Here White's older narrator makes up in a sense for having omitted one of his most profound relationships from many of his other fictions. Telling the story of Randall Worth, who seems to be based at least in part on White's ex-lover and lifelong friend, Stan Redfern, "Watermarked" explores the ways two young men from the Midwest "learned from the theater, improbably enough, . . . how to be gay" (254). Again, we discover in the tale some dominant themes in White's writing: gay life as something young men had to learn in the absence of healthy appreciations for homosexuality in 1950s and 1960s America, the endurance of friendship, and the persistence of love through friendship. Most important, the story makes a case for the transformative power of friends and lovers in one's life, the ways one's entire personality bears the imprint or watermark of the people one has loved. The story suggests that the past cannot be erased by age or disease.

"Pyrography" explores the erotics of desire in the triangular relationship between Otis, Danny, and Howard, whose explicit attraction to Danny only seemingly distinguishes him from the other boys. The story might be usefully read in relation to those moments in A Boy's Own Story when Kevin and his brother decide that novel's narrator is a "sissy." Like so much of White's work, it suggests that gay identity is not as coherent as it seems and that love between men is possible in a number of configurations.

Finally, "Skinned Alive," and "His Biographer," reflect, as does "Palace Days," White's experience in Paris, where he moved in 1983. "His Biographer" is a witty, if rather paranoid, examination of a man, Charles, who is a writer of biographies. But when someone offers to write the story of his life, Charles fears that his experience will be "forced into the mold of a traditional biography, a form in search of a trajectory, an imperative that produced a destiny" (111). Although Charles discovers that his biographer is incompetent, the tale's worry that a life cannot be reduced to a literary form gives us pause to think. What does it mean that White's stories attempt to do just that in portraying characters who would certainly be more complex as human beings than they are as literary creations? White (himself a master biographer) seems to challenge us to remember that good biography does not necessarily reflect a life truly and wholly. For that matter, neither does autobiographical fiction.

Perhaps the most demanding tale in the collection is the title story, "Skinned Alive," which concerns the dissolution of the narrator's relationship with Jean-Loup and his brief masochistic affair with Paul. The narrator is a writer, and the story provides, in some senses, a kind of authorial self-analysis. But rather than reassure us about the meaning of his life, the story shows the writer's failure to understand fully either Jean-Loup or Paul. In its broadest terms, "Skinned Alive" contrasts two ways of knowing about life—either abstractly, through ideas that interpret people and events, or by appreciating such people and events as they are. It is a theme revealed in a story within the story—an Ovidian tale of transformation Paul writes about the contest between Apollo, whose art is able to reveal "the contents of his mind," and the satyr Marsyas, who can copy "sacred lines" and "imitate a god as easily as a bawd," so long as his "model" is "there, in front of him" (81). The narrator initially interprets the story as an allegory about his own writing. He sees it either "as a reproach for having abandoned the Apollonian abstractness of [his] first two novels or, on the contrary, as an endorsement for undertaking [his] later satires and sketches" (82).

But the two ways of knowing detailed in the story also reflect the narrator's relationship to his two lovers, for with Paul he reveals himself to share a capacity for shaping reality through creative self-inscription that undermines his relationship to Jean-Loup. And with Jean-Loup, he engages in a provocative sexual relationship that he cannot seem to take at face value, for he keeps searching in it for meanings more profound or subtle than its obvious ones. The narrator's relationship with Paul and Paul's story act as rebukes to the narrator, whose own mental life and endless intellectual analysis overwhelm his love for both men, but especially Jean-Loup. As a result, the story ends wittily with the narrator's taking on a challenge Jean-Loup had earlier given him to describe his ass simply and directly, "in a style that was neither pornographic nor wimpy" (67). It is left up to the reader to understand how his witty prose poem succeeds or not on the level that Marsyas had succeeded, and whether or not his punishment will rekindle Jean-Loup's desire for him.

Christensen suggests that "Skinned Alive," especially its ending, demonstrates the "various epistemological strategies" the writer tries on "to see if there is anything to be learned from . . . unhappiness and humiliation."[15] He insists its narrator learns nothing that will lead him toward better relationships in the future. The analytic awareness he indulges with Paul simply makes him capable of more profound rationalizations. But that the narrator of "Skinned Alive" has so much difficulty knowing how to respond to his two lovers means that the reader does as well, and in a seminal article, Raymond-Jean Frontain argues this is a deliberate aspect of White's prose and narrative construction: "the final effect of the story's contradictions and paradoxes is the distillation within the narrator's voice of the experience of unknowing."[16] Frontain argues that White's autobiographical narrator provides the eye that sees in the story but not necessarily the key to understanding what he sees. We can never be certain—in this tale of masochistic submission—what constitutes love, and White's prose reveals but does not explain the "chaos and confusion" of his narrator's life.[17] If Frontain is correct, we might wonder if the same thing isn't true about many of the stories in White's collection. The characters in these stories are frequently at the center of perception, responding to the specific contexts of their lives and changing when that context does. But perhaps the meaning of what they say and do cannot finally be interpreted conclusively. If so, then White's stories certainly move toward the postmodern in their rejection of a coherent, unitary, and ultimately knowing and knowable subject.

The Married Man

Written shortly after *The Farewell Symphony, The Married Man* retraces events the narrator of the earlier novel left unspoken for the most part. As we saw, *The Farewell Symphony* begins with the death of the narrator's lover Brice from AIDS. But rather than tell that story, the narrative retreats nearly twenty years to talk about the narrator's life before AIDS. When the novel finally catches back up to the story of Brice, the narrator acknowledges that he simply cannot finish, and thus he breaks off. "I can't go on. I can't tell this story . . . ," he says.[18] It is not, apparently, that Brice's spirit cannot or does not deserve to be memorialized along with those of the others who have died of AIDS in the novel. On the contrary, the story is too personal, too much about the narrator himself: "I didn't want to think too much about him, nor about our life together, it had taken too much out of me, cost too much" (412). The response is credible, especially if we consider that Brice's story is an account of White's real-life relationship with Hubert Sorin, whom he met in 1989 and who died at age thirty-two on 17 March 1994 in Morocco. Nevertheless, in *The Married Man* White takes up that same personal and painful topic again, this time seeing it through from start to finish.

So, the differences between the two novels are key to understanding the later one. Typically White prefers first-person narration when he fictionalizes his experience. In his autobiographical trilogy, the first person rendered that experience immediate and enabled White to give voice to gay lives and characters in ways that had not been usual in American fiction before him. In *The Married Man*, White uses third-person narration, and what may at first seem a surprising return to a traditional style of narrative turns out to be a literary strategy for exploring the ways love binds two men so thoroughly that their separate identities merge through an "identification and a cross-identification" with one another.[19] Third-person narration helps us see, from an external point of view, how AIDS inevitably binds survivors to those who sicken and die. Lacking the narrative diffusion and immense range of sociological detail of *The Farewell Symphony*, *The Married Man* focuses in a unitary way on the love between its two main characters. Its chronological development emphasizes the inexorable and tragic progress of AIDS as it slowly decays the love the characters work to build.

Obviously, the story is not about *The Farewell Symphony*'s nameless narrator and Brice, but Austin and Julien. Austin is a forty-nine-year-old, HIV-positive American journalist and expert in French furniture of the eighteenth century who lives in Paris, where he meets and falls in love with Julien, a married man and architect in his late twenties. Soon after their meeting, Julien discovers not only that he, too, is infected with HIV, but that his infection has advanced into AIDS, the last stage of the illness. Describing the lovers' nearly five years together, *The Married Man* ends in death in Morocco, as did *The Farewell Symphony*. But we come to see that Austin himself has become the married man of the title and that what it means for a gay man to be connected so thoroughly to another is more complex than we might have imagined.

What is perhaps most remarkable about *The Married Man* is its integration of a rather traditional love story with what had become by the time White wrote the novel a conventional exposition of the accumulating horrors and degradations of AIDS. This exposition had reached a brilliant, if fevered, pitch in work such as Larry Kramer's play *The Normal Heart* (1985), Paul Monette's *Borrowed Time: An AIDS Memoir* (1988), and Monette's poems *Love Alone: Eighteen Elegies for Rog* (1988). These works mount "an aggressively blunt and harrowing assault" on the dominant culture's "denial of AIDS" in the 1980s.[20] *The Married Man*, however, is neither social nor political, but deeply personal, indeed tragic. With disciplined emotion, White reveals how nearly every forward step in the progress of Austin and Julien's love is accompanied by the disease. In the beginning, AIDS is nearly spectral, for although Austin is infected with HIV, he is—like White himself—one of those rare persons in whom the progress of the disease is slow or non-existent. He is not ill, and remains robustly healthy. He worries, however, about how to reveal his status to Julien, whom he presumes is HIV-negative. He fears Julien will leave him when he learns the truth, even though their sex has been scrupulously safe. Still, Julien declares his intention to stay with Austin despite his HIV status. "I realized you could—you *will*—become ill and it's a long illness," he says. "Anyway, I've decided I'm going to stay with you. I'll take care of you."[21]

By the end, however, it is Austin who is taking care of Julien, and the horrifying details of Julien's succumbing to AIDS are no longer spectral but fully embodied. The details are effective in themselves as evidence of human suffering and the frailty of life. They are clear signs written on Julien's body of the ways AIDS does and does not betray the men's love. When Julien is so ill he cannot stand up without assistance, he says to Austin, "Can't you see? It's over. Why won't you let me go?" But, Austin, "grim" and furious, can only say "I can't. I don't—" (290). So similar and yet so different from the words that ended this narrative in *The Farewell Symphony*, Austin's outburst seems to suggest that it is Julien and his love he cannot let go. The novel is not, then, an "AIDS novel" per se. It is a love story developed tragically, one in which AIDS marks the inevitable decline in circumstance through which we can come to understand the meaning and value of love itself. The novel reminds us that love persists even though the body inevitably fails. AIDS, paradoxically, points toward the value of something beyond that failure.

Because of the novel's sustained focus on a single love affair, White is able to explore the ethics of gay love relationships in *The Married Man* in greater detail than he has done before. White is always concerned in his work to represent accurately the nature of gay male relationships and the ways sex and friendship matter to them. Nevertheless, given that the kinds of love relationships White explores in his earlier novels are not necessarily defined in and around sexual monogamy or even sometimes sex itself, it can be difficult to see what exactly separates love from friendship in White's works (except perhaps the futility of longing for what cannot be had, as we saw in the two most important love relationships the narrator describes in *The Beautiful Room* and *The Farewell Symphony*, those with Sean and Kevin respectively). In *The Married Man* Austin and Julien's relationship proceeds like many another love story—gay or straight—on a trajectory through sex toward romance, "which Austin considered far more intimate and exciting," and on to commitment (108). Nevertheless the later life of their relationship is sexless. Austin stops having sex with Julien as a way of controlling tensions that emerge around his continuing friendship with his ex-lover Peter.

If such a settlement seems odd, we might recall that the dissociation of love from sex in *The Married Man* repeats a motif found in many of White's works (and we might remember as well that such a settlement is not unheard of in heterosexual marriage, although the reasons may or may not differ from the one's White explores here). For White, sex is "a pleasure, a communication, an appetite, an art"; it is not and should not be considered "our sole mode of transcendence" or "our only touchstone of authenticity."[22] So, although it can be part of love, it is not necessary to that experience and can be manipulated in a variety of relations to it. Serious, long-term gay relationships in White's works can be non-sexual, non-exclusive, and non-monogamous, that is, open relationships in which two men have multiple sex partners both within and outside their relationship. Love is not obligated to sexual desire, as in conventional accounts of romantic love.

Still, in *The Married Man* White makes clear that loving partners are bound by a mutual commitment to care for one another. For Austin at least, such relationships are not—in the manner of heterosexual marriage—construed as cordoning off the couple from other relations of friendship and obligation. Indeed, *The Married Man* explores the proposition that love and friendship necessarily blend within larger and more complex familial relations than those formed around the couple. This idea is not only apparent in the way Austin invites his friend Josephine to live with him and Julien when they briefly relocate to Providence, Rhode Island, where Austin gets a teaching position. It is also the focus of one of the few sustained subplots within the novel, one that describes the relationship between Austin and his ex-lover, Peter. He, too, is positive, and although Peter has long since moved back to America, he visits Austin in Paris, travels frequently with Austin, and with Austin and Julien as well. It is Austin's sense that Peter may have to move in with him and Julien when his health begins to deteriorate from AIDS.

What we see embodied here is the same strand of familial solicitude that primarily defines Austin and Julien's relationship, one Austin takes as a defining gesture of gay relationships. He says that "gay men . . . should stay loyal to their old friends and lovers and take them in when necessary, not reject their former mates like heartless heterosexuals" (104). So strong is his feeling that, when Julien demurs, Austin makes the decision to stop having sex with him. Austin denounces him for having "bad heterosexual values. As the new wife he, Julien, assumed he had the right to insist that Austin never talk to the ex-wife, Peter. . . . Only heterosexuals could be so cruel; among male homosexuals friendship ruled supreme" (177).

So although the novel shows that values such as Austin's might lead to jealousy, Julien himself is represented as having an unbecoming replacement model of love and affection, one he demonstrated when he was willing to give up his wife Christine to live with Austin and one he seems to expect Austin to imitate with Peter. *The Married Man*, then, introduces a healthy dose of skepticisim about the supposed superiority of heterosexual to homo-sexual relationships, and it represents gay love in rich complexity, as a fluid combination of sex, love, and friendship. Revealing these differences as if they need no apology represents a full flowering of the gay American novel, which no longer seeks simple redress of grievance for its gay characters but, in some ways, an accounting by heterosexual society for its own failure to develop more inclusionary social models of sex and love.

One of the great pleasures of reading *The Married Man* is its focus on the differences between life in France and America, in particular the ways gay life and identity are imagined by two different cultures. In some senses, the gay people and communities represented in White's novels have been conceived on the model of an ethnic American identity. Their identities are formed at least in part through their collective struggle for social legitimacy and politi-cal rights. Gay thinkers have debated the utility of this idea on many levels in recent years, and it is not clear that White's own emphasis on the creative self-invention of gay people in American life is wholly consistent with such politicized models of identity. Still, as we saw in *The Farewell Symphony*, White's celebration of the gay life of New York in the 1970s was based in no small part on the way it enabled a tremendous explosion of creative energy through gay men's being released from the homophobia and sterility of life in middle-class America.

The Married Man models other, French, ways of arranging one's sexual affairs—most notably in the bisexuality many of Austin's French lovers cling to. "I had no problem accepting the idea of being gay," Julien says, "but it wasn't black and white for me" (31). It is an admission that leads Austin to reconsider his own "West Village smugness; he had belonged to a New York gay world for twenty years and it had left him with too many ready answers" (32). What seems most to distinguish French, or at least Julien's, attitudes toward sexuality is the insistence that it ought not place one in a marginal, group relation to society. "Julien believed he shared nothing with other gay men. In fact he rejected all group identity" (92).

It is precisely Austin's American smugness, however, that leads him to misunderstand, even underestimate one aspect of Julien's character that links him to any number of White's self-inventing gay characters. When Austin and Julien first meet, Julien suggests to Austin that he is from a privileged background, although he remains completely evasive about the details. Austin takes him at face value, so that when Julien asserts his difference from other gay men and his "independence of spirit," Austin can attribute it solely to a minor aristocrat's imagination of his own self-invention. "Julien thought he'd invented himself, whereas Austin saw him as simply an unusual recombination of herd traits" (92). But at the end, in the final chapter, which sums up the novel after Julien's death, we discover that Julien is from a solidly working-class family, that he has had periods of promiscuous gay living, and that he has engaged in his affairs with an unusual cast of characters. It is a revelation for Austin. Julien had, in fact, invented himself, with the result that he gets what he wants—"the big, glamorous life" that Austin can provide (310).

These revelations raise a number of unanswered questions: Was Julien aware he might be infected with HIV in the first place and so ready to settle down with a man who knew the ropes? Was his rejection of gay identity a position rehearsed only after a life of sexual abandon as a gay man? And were his pretensions to aristocratic status a ploy to catch Austin, whose own American class consciousness led him to see Julien as his entrée into an "upper-class French life" that offered "the exact shade of inclusion he had craved for" (91)?

Whatever the answers to these questions, the novel tends to corroborate a theme we have discovered in White's other works: "Between two men . . . no union could ever be a matter of course. Everything had to be invented, reimagined . . ." (91). If Austin mistakes his relationship with Julien as being the exception, because Julien seems to represent some kind of imaginary authenticity Austin has been seeking, the novel ends with a reappraisal of Julien that may explain on an even more profound level what his attractions were: his ability to raise people above their lackluster origins by reimagining them on the "stage" of his consciousness (309).

This gift, after all, is precisely what Julien gives to Austin, who is fully transformed by their love. "It was as if they'd fused, as if Julien had been an alien who'd snatched his body, encoded his nervous system and changed his blood type, colonized his organs and rescripted his memory bank. . . . The only thing that still belonged to him, that resembled his old self, was his face, his arms and legs, his body, but they, too, had been impaired by this devastating inner metamorphosis" (309–10). It is not the first time in White's work that we have seen love figured as a disease that transfigures the body. Here, however, it signifies the identification of lovers in relation to and through the virus that brings them together and holds them apart, so that we might properly say the novel boldly reimagines the HIV virus itself as something more than a simple harbinger of death. It seems rather to be another location around which gay men can and have reinvented themselves.

In this sense, we also might recognize the importance of White's thinking about AIDS outside its obvious medical and tragic meanings. *The Married Man* explores the various illogicalities of efforts to understand the causes of AIDS. The novel worries the question of Julien's infection, but it does not do so in sterile pursuit of trying to settle the vexed and usually mysterious relationship between sexual activity and disease. On the contrary, it suggests that causal understandings are bound to fail in revealing the human costs of or solutions to the tragedy.

Certainly Austin spends a good deal of the novel worrying that he may have been the source of Julien's infection, and at the end, in his delirium and unhappiness, Julien himself accuses Austin. More than an honest statement of fact, however, it is likely that the accusation simply helps characterize Julien's helplessness or that it is his way of trying to wean Austin from the relationship that is ending. The circumstances of the novel make it highly unlikely that Austin gave Julien the disease, which Julien's doctors confirm. Instead the novel demonstrates the many, including cultural, conditions around which HIV transmission occurs. So, Julien is a Frenchman reluctant to identify himself as gay, which could suggest a degree of denial about his sexual involvement with men prior to his meeting Austin. But we also learn that Julien had been injected with an unsterilized needle when he lived in Ethiopia, which may be as likely a source of infection as unsafe sex in France. And despite having sex with Julien, his wife Christine remains HIV-negative.

What such conflicting evidence suggests is that it is difficult to know except in the most general of ways what may have caused any individual case of AIDS. That people like Austin continue to worry about the issue suggests that questions of causality are, for gay men at least, unanswerable questions of survivor's guilt. Austin "feared he'd been the one to infect Julien" (161). Austin has survived the death of almost all his gay friends of his own age, and he survives the death of two of his younger lovers, Peter and Julien. Guilt seems an all-too-human response: "Some days Austin hoped that he would fall down a manhole or double over from a heart attack the day after he buried Julien. That would all be so much simpler. In that case he wouldn't have to rebuild a new life. The tackiness of survival—which led, inevitably, to forgetting and faithlessness—could be obviated" (243). But White makes clear here that survivor's guilt morphs into something ever so slightly different: a feeling of betrayal. Life after the death of a loved one, many loved ones, involves moving on, finding new ways to live without the lover, and so constitutes a kind of faithlessness. In fact, Austin acknowledges that this moving on is a process that begins even before death: "he knew that the minute someone became ill he began, secretly, to withdraw larger and larger sums of love from that person's account" (161–62).

It is in just such admissions that the novel reveals the tremendous toll AIDS takes on those who survive it. And it is in such admissions that the novel recognizes that life continues despite AIDS. In reviewing *The Married Man* for England's *The Guardian,* James Hopkins noted that "White's interweaving of opposites and his readiness to view the many sides of every attitude save the novel from sentimentality or survivor guilt."[23] Here, in Austin's unsentimental gesture, we see White's determination to present AIDS in the realistic if paradoxical light of human mortality and persistence—not in the sentimentalities of moralists or the scientific platitudes of medicine.

CHAPTER FOUR

Early, Experimental Fiction

Forgetting Elena, Nocturnes for the King of Naples, and *Caracole*

Perhaps White's most challenging novels are three he wrote early in his career—two before *A Boy's Own Story* and one immediately afterwards. White has said that *Forgetting Elena* was substantially finished as early as 1969, although it was not published for another four years. The delay may have been due to its muted though evident allusions to gay life on Fire Island in the 1960s, but it is just as likely to have been the result of White's struggling to master its striking formal experiments.[1] *Nocturnes for the King of Naples* was published five years later, in 1978, becoming one of the first American novels written about explicitly gay characters and themes to be published by a mainstream American press. And *Caracole*, White's so-called "heterosexual" novel because it has no gay characters, appeared in 1985.

Although it is not their most important dimension, all three novels bear traces of the autobiographical impulse that dominates White's writing. *Forgetting Elena* concerns a young man trying to discover his own elusive identity in a subtle and sophisticated society that seems entirely new to him—a situation White has said echoed his own journey from the American Midwest to the rarified social and intellectual world of New York in the 1960s. In *Nocturnes* White describes an unrequited love similar to one he experienced for a young actor, Keith McDermott, in the 1970s. In an interesting twist, White narrates the story in the voice of the young man who rejects his distinguished, older lover, a character who, White has said, was modeled both on the gay American poet Frank O'Hara and himself. And *Caracole* is a baroque tale of love lost and found based loosely on events surrounding the coming of White's nephew Keith Fleming to live with his uncle in New York in the 1970s. The novel has also been seen as a roman à clef peopled with the easily identifiable New York intellectuals with whom White was friendly in the 1970s, people such as Richard Howard, Susan Sontag, and Richard Sennett.

All three novels are linked by their concern for a young character who finds himself in a sophisticated, intellectual world or a world of intriguing new sexual opportunity—in White's work these often overlap. However, whereas White's autobiographical novels explore such themes in terms of the personal development of an individual—over the course of his autobiographical trilogy a repressed boy from the Midwest comes to New York and discovers a productive gay identity, a gay community to live in, and love—the earlier, experimental novels are more concerned with analyzing the nature of the societies in which their young characters find themselves. Or they are focused on the sometimes debilitating introspection that results from a confrontation with such super-sophisticated worlds. In this emphasis, they reflect European and French models, especially those of White's favorite authors, Vladimir Nabokov and Marcel Proust, rather than the dominant social realism of the English and American novelistic traditions. The three novels are united as well by their style and form. In all three, White creates highly particular structures and elaborate prose styles to reveal his characters not simply as individuals in confrontation with society but as subjects who only come into being through their interactions with that society.

Forgetting Elena

Forgetting Elena is a case in point. Although White cautioned David Bergman that the setting of the novel "was only very approximately Fire Island," he nevertheless conceded that to the extent he had a specific location in mind, it was Fire Island Pines.[2] But if Bergman rightly asserts that "it would be a mistake to tie the allegorical [aspects of the novel] too tightly to the real Fire Island," he also identifies an "unreal" quality about the actual location that overlaps productively with the setting imagined by White.[3] White's novel mythologizes a subculture peculiar to that emerging on Fire Island in the 1960s, and it does so by way of exploring new sexually and socially permissive cultures emerging in middle-class American life at that time. Fire Island, then, is a good place to start in understanding the novel.

A thin strip of land off the southern coast of Long Island, Fire Island and its pristine beaches have long been a summer vacation ground for wealthy people from Manhattan—including gay men. Wealthy residents owned or rented houses where they could stay for the whole of the summer, and in the 1960s and 1970s urban gay residents of Manhattan left Penn Station every weekend and vacation period and flocked to Sayville, where they took the ferry across the bay to enjoy themselves in expensive rented bungalows shared by groups whose size depended on how much each individual member could afford to spend. Fire Island became synonymous in emerging gay communities across America with a leisured, sexually open lifestyle. Its mythology was enhanced both by the many hotels and beach establishments in locations such as Cherry Grove where gay men could dance throughout the long, hot summer nights and the infamous dunes at Fire Island Pines where they cruised for sex in the open air. Although White has written in *City Boy*, his memoir about life in the 1970s, that gay life even on Fire Island was subject to its own forms of homophobic scrutiny by the police, a younger gay crowd mixed with older gay and straight established residents of the island to create a tense (if also utopian) integration of different gay lifestyles with more traditional ones. It is this situation that provides the premise of *Forgetting Elena*, for the novel explores the ways the new, seemingly more permissive social ethics of the 1960s were changing the fabric of social interaction among America's leisured classes—gay and straight.

On one level, *Forgetting Elena* is a fairly straightforward account of the tensions that emerge in any community when a new social ethic replaces another more traditional one. The novel explores these tensions in the transformation from an "Old Code," dominated by Doris and the Valentine family, whose history becomes important to the nameless narrator of the novel, and a "New Code" devised and policed by Herbert and his friends, a group of men the narrator awakens to find himself living among at the opening of the work. Each faction vies for the loyalty of the narrator, who is, apparently, an important person. Doris's faction is associated with an older lifestyle that exists side-by-side with Herbert's "New Code" but that nevertheless is quickly losing ground.[4] White wittily characterizes this tradition through reference to its rather old-fashioned habits—drinking Campari in the evening before going out to eat on "silver trays burdened with black roasts" across which are "scattered . . . thin sheets of edible silver leaf" (117). The "Old Code" is all "clumsy pomp," or at least it seems so to admirers of the new (168). It espouses a hierarchy of people symbolized by the magnificent mansions in which many of the old guard seem to live, although in the novel's opening chapter the last of the great mansions on the novel's fictional island has been burned down with deliberation it seems by agents unknown. Under the New Code, hierarchies or "'first' families" are—ostensibly—no longer to be, and the end of the great houses seemingly makes way for more modest cottages that house people in more egalitarian situations (83). As Herbert says early in the book, "we're all equals now" (7). His words are a clue to the egalitarian pretensions of the New Code.

Nevertheless life in Herbert's cottage is perhaps more carefully regulated than ever, except that the criterion for evaluation, as Harry Mathews points out, is now aesthetic.[5] The point is well illustrated by the portentous, albeit hilarious opening sentence of the novel, when the narrator wakes up in Herbert's cottage on what will become a beautiful summer morning: "I am the first person in the house to awaken, but I am unsure of the implications" (3). Ordinarily one might consider what one is going to do with the day when one wakes, but White's narrator ponders the meaning of his awakening, as if he were not a person but a text to be expounded by his own, in this case inept, interpretation. As the narrator stumbles through his morning, he is obsessed with knowing how to behave in this house of men: what is the right thing to do and when? What is the appropriate thing to say? "I wonder what sort of impression I might make if I should go to the bathroom now?" (4). Obviously, the tone is arch and ironic, meant to be droll. But the situation seems ominous as well. While Herbert's new world declares itself part of a freer sexual and social order, in many ways, as we will see, "the New Code simply repeats the old oppressive structures in disguised form."[6]

Herbert is a mysterious, tyrannical figure who rules his cottage-world absolutely by inculcating a respect for the rules of a new order that he alone seems to have mastered. Every utterance made in his company, every action, no matter how small, becomes a test of one's mastery of the new aesthetics. One member of the household comments on another, Bob, for leaving the dinner table too early to go dancing at the hotel disco: "Dance? How absurd! No one ever goes to the hotel until the stroke of midnight" (4). The unnamed speaker chastises Bob for being literal minded, for wanting to understand exactly when one can or cannot do things in order to maintain decorum. The key to knowing what to do, a key Bob apparently lacks, is to "scrutinize the mood of the crowd, keep [an] eye on important people, observe when *they* appear to be restless and likely to leave" (5). Herbert claims to be too respectful of individual freedoms to criticize Bob for "lacking in the social instincts." "Who needs them?" he asks (5).

But he adroitly turns the conversation to Bob's "other, more important qualities" and, in doing so, patronizes Bob for his otherwise inept mannerisms that Herbert deems to be "charming." "Today I isolated a new mannerism in Bob: shall I call it the 'yawning syndrome'?" "The 'yawning syndrome' occurs whenever Bob feels ill-at-ease, uncertain of going or coming, or when he's aware of some tension he may have provoked in the company" (5). Herbert initially appears as one with his guests as he joins in the ridicule of Bob's social failures; however, he manipulates the conversation so that he comes out the master of nuance and the ultimate arbiter of social value. When another member of the household picks up on Herbert's ridicule, he asks in mock exasperation, "Why do we put up with Bob?"(6), and then proceeds to judge Bob's fashion lapses in a manner reminiscent of Herbert's chastising his mannerisms. But Herbert challenges him: "'Why do we put up with Bob?' I would have thought nothing would be easier to do. He's a charming young man" (7). The original speaker of the question is now, the narrator informs us, "in disgrace" (8).

It seems clear that Bob's attractions are his youth and charm, perhaps his physical beauty. Under the New Code, one's social place seems to be negotiated through the combination of one's physical attractiveness, one's mastery of aesthetics of one sort or another, and one's intuition of and adherence to otherwise unstated social norms. Most important of all, though, is the ability to observe and evaluate others without appearing to judge them, which is the mistake, it seems, of the man who is disgraced by asking why he and his housemates put up with Bob. *Forgetting Elena* wittily sends up this new, only seemingly egalitarian social order in which there is no room for judgment but no end to the refinement of social and aesthetic taste exercised in the evaluation of oneself and, more importantly, others. As Les Brookes suggests, what is lost to this new social order is a genuine feeling for people's needs and emotions, or any support for their differences.[7]

One thing that has caused a great deal of worry in critical interpretations of *Forgetting Elena* is that it does not deal precisely with its characters' sexual orientations, and in this very specific sense does not seem to be a gay novel. White himself has said that "*Forgetting Elena* was the first book I had written that wasn't gay," although he later qualified his point by saying that he "wanted to tap the energies of homosexuality without drawing an explicit portrait of its folkways."[8] The novel's critics have identified gay elements in the novel or not, depending primarily on their specific investment in gay politics.[9] Nevertheless it seems relatively clear that Herbert notices Bob's physical charm, and as we will see he also seems to be one of the narrator's lovers (a point White confirms as well).[10] Given that the underlying conflict in the novel is balanced provocatively between the male homosocial world of Herbert's "New Code" and the traditional familial structure of Doris's "Old" one, the novel challenges us at the very least to be alert to the possible ways new gay social relationships and sexual ethics shape its world.

Indeed, for Stephen Barber "the novel is finally about the urgent creation and simultaneous cancellation or deferral of a language for gay identity," while for David Bergman it reflects the experience of gay men at a time "when gay social life was much more cut off from mainstream America and operated in its own unfamiliar and often inscrutable codes of conduct."[11] And Les Brookes understands the novel as a critique of a gay leisured class emerging on Fire Island in the 1970s, a class unresponsive to calls for a widespread liberation of sexuality.[12] Clearly, then, *Forgetting Elena* explores a perceived ethics evolving in gay and other liberatory sexual movements in the 1960s and 1970s that sought alternatives to the moral structures traditionally regulating sex. In this sense, it assuredly qualifies as a gay novel.

Still, what is perhaps most fascinating about *Forgetting Elena* and what makes it one of White's most difficult works are its literary experiments with the conventions of the novel. White combines the novel of manners, a genre that portrays the customs and manners of a highly complex society, with the bildungsroman, a traditional form that chronicles the moral and psychological growth of a young character. Its narrator, like so many others in White's novels, is nameless, and we might expect that as the novel progresses he will come to understand himself more complexly and achieve an identity. But to a large extent White frustrates these expectations. Rather than discover who he is, White's narrator seems to be involved in the arduous task of forgetting who he was.

Not simply an unreliable narrator, he is an amnesiac who spends the novel seeking clues to his identity—although it might also be reasonably inferred that the narrator no longer knows who he is because it has been useful or expedient for someone, perhaps the narrator himself, to forget the answer to that question. The narrator awakens in a house—Herbert's cottage —in which he seems barely acquainted with the other inhabitants and lacks a full understanding of his social role in being there. By the end he is revealed to occupy a quite privileged role among the inhabitants of the island where Doris and Herbert compete for control. We discover he is "a prince, *the* prince" of the island (178). But that social role does not necessarily bring him self-awareness in any of the usual senses of the phrase. Thus White, provocatively, separates his narrator's identity from his social role, suggesting perhaps that who the narrator is is less important than the role he plays.

Forgetting Elena also lacks a plot per se. If its narrator is not a character whose complex identity emerges at the end, then it would seem unnecessary to show him growing through a series of clearly interrelated actions—the traditional form of the bildungsroman. Like the French *nouveau roman*, White's work eschews a structure that shapes the reader's comprehension of the novel's subject as an objectively comprehended totality. Instead, *Forgetting Elena* is structured as a series of episodes in which the narrator attempts to recall his past but only ends up deepening our sense of the mysteries of his social role and identity.

Although the narrator lives with Herbert, his relationship to the older man is not entirely clear. Herbert is certainly some kind of older friend or guardian, but he may also be, as we've seen, the narrator's lover. He sets pointless tasks for the young man—asking him, for instance, to clear the pine needles that have fallen into the sand around a building mysteriously called the "Detached Residence" (31)—and the narrator childishly rebels, first by masturbating in the sand and then by joining a mysterious young woman on a walk up the beach in the middle of the day. This walk becomes a procession of hangers on (some of them important people under the Old Code), and one that takes on immense significance in this world in which behavior is constantly observed and judged for its novelty and social posturing. It comes to be celebrated as "the Little Stroll" (53), and it seems to portend some kind of change in social relations for the narrator.

The woman, it turns out is Elena Valentine, seemingly a member of the social faction dominated by Doris and opposed to Herbert and the supporters of the New Code. So the narrator's rebellion might seem to be leading to a break from Herbert. The narrator goes to Elena's house, where she reads from a "sort of . . . history of the Valentines" (70), before the two become involved in a short-lived sexual partnership. Elena's history of her family seems extraordinarily suggestive about the narrator's identity, but rather comically—even pathetically—he can't figure out whether he is Elena's brother, her former lover, or both. It would seem that he is at least a former lover and that at some time in the past Herbert has come between the two.

But after several significant episodes of soul searching in which the narrator has a drink with Doris and performs what he takes to be a provocative, solo dance at the disco (one in which he asserts his independence from and mastery of all others), the narrator reunites with Herbert. The two men write poems that suggest their love for one another or, at the least, recognize their intimacy through their mutual esteem for love as a value—in a world so precious, one in which authenticity has ceased to be, simple spoken declarations of emotion seem all but impossible. Even so, as the novel moves toward its conclusion, Herbert makes an ominous announcement: "Elena killed herself last night" (169). If what Herbert says is true, her action would seem to fulfill a prediction written into her memoir, and thus provide some coherence and credibility to a plot that seems doubtfully motivated. "Perhaps you will come back . . . ," she had written, "you'll return only for a night or two or three and then leave me again. If that should happen, I don't think I could go on living" (175).

Read one way, the novel might seem to be a melodramatic rendering of a triangular relationship that ends in suicide or worse. But things are more complex than that. The truth is we do not receive sufficient, unambiguous information in the novel to confirm Elena's death, and Herbert obviously uses the report of it to try to consolidate his hold on the narrator. Elena certainly disappears as a literal character, but rather than become an occasion for anyone (except perhaps the narrator) to grieve, her purported death is transformed into a symbol for what must be forgotten if the narrator is to take his place in the "New Order" that the now-aligned Herbert and Doris have conceived to supersede the "New Code" (158).

Whether or not Elena literally dies seems irrelevant. Because this is not a realistic novel, White doesn't sort out the plausible motives of her actions. Instead, he shows that the report of her death can become another example of the way people, events, and narratives are manipulated to function symbolically and ritually in this super-sophisticated world. Like a stroll on the beach that becomes fraught with social significance, a memoir that recalls events its participants can't (or won't) confirm, and devotional poems that always already mean something else, the report of the death of a major character is transformed into a symbol open to interpretation and re-signification. What makes *Forgetting Elena* especially difficult is that it doesn't always give us a way to judge effectively the validity of the characters' usually self-serving interpretations of the novel's events. The plot seems less a coherent narrative grounded in empirical reality than a contest among the island's various inhabitants to control their own and others' understanding of a reality open to constant re-inscription. In particular, it represents a struggle between Elena and Herbert, and between the both of them and the narrator, to define and control the narrator's place, meaning, and identity.

Even the conclusion, in which we might hope to find some resolution to the problems posed by the plot, is ambiguous. Although *Forgetting Elena* clearly takes place in a modern world, the ending of the novel stages a feudal ceremony referred to as the "Royal Arrival" (168), a type of coronation ritual in which the narrator assumes his role as prince. How literally we are to take this ceremony, and what power it conveys to the narrator, is not entirely evident. Elena describes this investiture as an "old" form revived so that it can be "filled with new content" by Herbert and his social faction (168), who apparently seek control of the island through their mastery of social forms.

The feudal metaphor would seem to characterize tellingly the structures of authority on the island, even as the ceremony itself restages and presumably settles the conflicts of its powerful inhabitants. By this point Herbert has aligned himself with Doris—both apparently, seeking to enhance their power among the island's citizens and both banishing Elena from their company before her purported death. And Herbert takes on yet another role, this time as "Regent" (180), the person supposedly put in place by the narrator's now-dead father to guide the young man toward his important role as "*the prince*" of the island (78). But although this new designation seems to institutionalize Herbert's hold on the young man by confirming his legitimacy as a father-substitute, it may also designate his formal subservence to the "prince," whose "arrival" could consolidate or threaten Herbert's control. So, even the conclusion, wrapped as it is in a feudal metaphor denoting new hierarchies and modes of control, doesn't settle the question of who will become the ultimate arbiter of social form and meaning on the island.

As for the narrator, "the prince," the Royal Arrival would seem to show his coming into his own. Because the novel arrives at a ceremony seeming to invest him with an adult position in the world, it could convey a sense of growth and psychological maturation. Perhaps it prepares him for a brave new future projected at the end of the novel. Given, however, that the Arrival ends with the narrator evacuating his memory of as least some of his former social relations if not his entire identity, it is just as likely that the ceremony in which he becomes a prince is little more than a self-aggrandizing fantasy of self-awareness and self-possession disguising the young man's role in the various shifts of power that have been enacted throughout.

Because part of the ceremony of the "Royal Arrival" seems to be for the incoming prince to perform a ritual burial of something that is "a symbol of what the Prince might regret or wish to forget" (168), Elena's demise (real or imaginary) could not be more convenient. It seems to be her body that is buried in the closing pages, along with the narrator's memory of her and his former life on the island. "Is there a dead person in that box? Am I a newcomer to the island? I remember nothing. Who is Elena?" (184). In this regard, *Forgetting Elena* can be read as a record of the narrator's casting off old alliances—symbolized by his love for Elena and her apparent involvement in his family history—to become the blank slate he seems to be at the conclusion. That he loved Elena at one time now seems clear. As part of the Royal Arrival, the narrator enters the Detached Residence, which he now vaguely recognizes as his boyhood home. When he enters his old bedroom he spontaneously remembers—for the first and only time in the novel—his youthful love for Elena as well as a mournful song he used to enjoy about a couple whose happiness is destroyed when the man leaves for reasons he can't remember (182).

Perhaps Elena is not an appropriate mate for a "prince," and Herbert's guardianship has been established by the narrator's father to assure that his son forgets her. Or perhaps Herbert has abused his power in removing the narrator from Elena, so that he can assume greater control of the island. That reading makes sense given that the primary tension of the novel proceeds from the struggle between the two social factions headed by Herbert and Doris. If the narrator's forgetting Elena is a calculated effort on his part to remove himself from his past, to begin again from scratch as it were, then the novel could also be something of an allegory of a young man's transition from a heterosexual world into a homosexual one, or from any conventional social world to another, newer one. The novel simply does not adjudicate definitively among multiple tantalizing possibilities.

But however we interpret the tensions of the novel's conclusion, one thing does seem clear. White's narrator is both devious and improvisational. His subterfuges and self-satisfactions are not unlike those of the narrator of *A Boy's Own Story*, for he is capable of betrayal and, worse, forgetting those he has betrayed, and he is brilliant at devising responses to the new social sensations thrown at him. In its portrait of the narrator, the novel seems to offer up a prescription for a type of absolute power: the ability to forget everything but what conduces to one's present fantasy for an assured place in an unsure world. What we think of that power—whether we think it is good or not—depends on what we think of the world White has described.

In understanding *Forgetting Elena*, then, we might recognize that the work's unconventional characterization and seemingly unstructured plot are strategies White uses to point toward the narrator's arrival at a unsettling state, one in which he is poised to create himself wholly anew, out of nothingness as it were, in a world that fetishizes novelty and social improvisation. Indeed, the peculiar construction of the novel allows White to achieve what a more realistic novel might not: a convincing portrait of a world in which the apprehension of reality is shaped through the manipulation of social and aesthetic forms rather than empirical understanding. It is a world at once frightening and replete with possibilities.

Like White's autobiographical novels, *Forgetting Elena* is modernist in its exploration of an individual's attempt to achieve coherence in response to social worlds revealed only in the limited perspective of one's fragmented perceptions. In *City Boy*, White says that he had been "reading Kafka and Beckett" when he wrote *Forgetting Elena*, and the impact of both writers' tragicomic realization of how human identity is shaped by a limited social and metaphysical understanding seems fundamental to it (56). Indeed, the novel is a witty if troubling response to the great modernist novelist White admires perhaps more than any other, Marcel Proust, whose *In Search of Lost Time* explores the sentience and pleasures of individuals as these emerge in response to involuntary memories recalling their formative past. In White's novel the present becomes the only direct source of one's experience, so under Herbert's new social ethic the most pleasurable sensations may be the ones that emerge out of forgetfulness. White has written in *City Boy* that he wanted to show that we are always "modeling our behavior on the expectations of those around us and the cues we were being fed. The self was a social self; at our core lay a reciprocity," an idea he attributes to the sociologist Erving Goffman (57).

But *Forgetting Elena* seems to move beyond Goffman's notion that we define ourselves through a type of theatrical role-playing by gesturing toward a postmodern lack of faith in the self's ability to be merely sincere and purely authentic. It may even suggest that the self, like experience, is textual, that is, constructed through rather than having an ontological being prior to the languages and discourses that shape knowledge of it.

J. D. McClatchy has written that the novel is "a literally artificial world, whose characters are names, whose details are nouns, whose plot is semiotic, whose subject is fiction, and so its tragi-comedy of manners is finally about style itself."[13] Its surface narrative about a prince searching for his own identity, McClatchy suggests, may reflect the author's own struggle to find a voice, the proper blend of irony, satire, and celebration of what was new in the life he was living in gay New York in 1969. Certainly the narrator's dance toward the end of the novel suggests that it is only by learning to perform one's self separately from others that one becomes a self at all. If this is true, it might explain the aesthetic and rhetorical significance of the novel's being written in the first person, entirely in the present. Literally the narrator must speak about himself in the present because he knows no past. The novel records his experience of becoming even as it unfolds. The narrator, in effect, writes himself, and so emerges as a prince.

On this level, the novel seems to position the rejected Elena on one side of a defining issue of modernist ethics: the question of sincerity and individual authenticity that emerged in the existentialist thought dominant in the several decades following World War II. Elena's memoir rejects the ironies of Herbert's New Code in favor of the "adventure in sincerity" she shares with "the perfect man," who is, presumably, the narrator (173). "We were different," she writes. "We weren't parading delicate perceptions. In the evening we spent hours confessing the secrets we had hidden an entire lifetime, and we weren't ashamed to be only human" (172–73). Her words reject Herbert's preference for negotiating emotion and human interaction through aesthetic forms, the most obvious of which are the poems he and the narrator write to bring them into more intimate connection around any number of personally or socially compelling situations throughout the novel.

The narrator doesn't necessarily agree, as his ultimate rejection of Elena implies. Admittedly, during the Royal Arrival he does comment on the decorum of the gardens surrounding the Detached Residence in words that seem to reflect Elena's rejection of the aesthetic: "I'd have been happier with a yard full of plaster flamingos, happier with less taste and more humanity" (180).[14] But these sentiments may be weighted paradoxically against his earlier assertion that writing poems is a way "to invent sincerity" at moments when the body, independent of the will, feels emotion in the form of a "clenched stomach" (171). He seems to suggest that there are real emotions signaled at the level of the body, but that one only understands them through aesthetic analysis. "I don't trust my body," he continues. "Left to its own devices the body won't come through," and so one has to rely on artifice: "Pills and poems are called for; a purge for the bowels; a poem to facilitate the search for experience" (171). The body exists; one's experience of it is textual, that is, its meaning and significance are understood, explored, negotiated, and shaped through words.

Such ideas seem almost as if they belong to a treatise on poststructuralism. Roland Barthes was writing at the same time as White was producing his early novels, and White was reading him, so perhaps they do. But the idea certainly propels *Forgetting Elena* into the postmodern future of its writing, for the novel goes even further than McClatchy suggests in exploring the textuality of experience. It may suggest that the self is merely a rhetorical marker in the play of language, a sign signifying the possibilities for meaning that are never constituted as the self alone but only in relation to those infinite Others—people and objects—through which one's understanding of self is always made contingent.

As he walks on the beach one night toward the close of the novel, the narrator compares himself to "water, sand and sky" that are "dispersed by the wind" (which he earlier called "the animating soul of the world"): "I'm a carousel of possibilities turning on emptiness. But someone might say something to me. I might answer. My answer exists. One remark produces another. Now we have something to go on. Statements to reconcile, consistency to maintain, inventions to elaborate. Features emerge, waves gather, a dune dries, crumbles and slides" (132–33). Although White refers his novel to the sociologist Erving Goffman's understanding that one constructs oneself socially through the roles one plays, here his narrator seems to reject the theatrical metaphor underlying Goffman's ideas. He doesn't imagine himself playing a role so much as inventing himself out of emptiness. He is open to possibilities that are evoked in language and that, like the ocean and its dunes, are always in flux. There remains something of the older, existentialist ethic in White's protagonist, a faith that one creates oneself through the choices one makes. But as this moment suggests, the novel begins to move beyond these older notions toward more poststructuralist ones. The narrator seems to intuit that his self is composed around an essential "emptiness."

The French psychoanalyst Jacques Lacan imagined an early stage of subjectivity in infants' recognition of themselves in a mirror that reflected back to them not their self but an image of a "total form" and the presentiment of a "maturation" of "power" that can only be a fantasy because it is not them.[15] The mirror stage in Lacanian psychoanalysis is a moment of primordial misrecognition that anticipates the later emergence of alienated subjectivity. In other words, for Lacan, the individual subject is not self-identical in the way of the Cartesian cogito ("I think, therefore I am"), but recognizes itself primarily through the gaze of an Other, who represents what the subject is not. Subjectivity, then, is constituted as a lack rather than an originary fullness of being. Although White is scathingly dismissive of Lacan in his autobiography, *My Lives*,[16] the psychoanalyst's ideas are helpful in this context, for the famous mirror stage is recalled in *Forgetting Elena* when the narrator walks into the bathroom of a disco. Upon entering, he says "a full-length mirror hangs on the far wall and I watch my reflection approach me—no, it's Herbert, it's not a mirror. I had forgotten what I look like" (122).

Mirrors in the novel, Harry Mathews rightly points out, gesture symbolically toward "the responsive gaze of others [that] certifies an individual's existence."[17] But Lacan helps us see something more in this moment: Herbert is not simply an Other who certifies the narrator's existence but the Other who reminds him of who he is not. As does the whole novel, this moment signifies the narrator's comprehension of (and apprehension at) his lack of being—not the authenticity of his self but the nothingness signified by his recognizing himself primarily through what he is not. The point is not that Lacan influenced White, but that the experimentation with form in White's work itself opens new frameworks for understanding the interrelation of society and self that were also being explored in other contemporary contexts.

Just as we cannot easily corroborate the accuracy of Herbert's announcement of Elena's death, the ambiguous evidence of her memoir, or the truth about the narrator's role or identity, we also cannot confirm the words in White's novel. The novel is an invention and fantasy of its narrator, in which he looks to the aesthetic meaning of events or other texts for confirmation of his uncertain identity and ends up concocting a seemingly powerful social role out of the rituals he enacts and the words he speaks—always in the present of his experience. The past, if it exists at all, exists to be re-invented by a man who cannot remember who he is. And the future is a possibility disburdened of its connection to the past because it is always open to creative re-invention. This point is important because the narrator recognizes that history can be a trap when it is treated as a source or origin to explain who one is in the present. It becomes a text from which one cannot escape. On the afternoon when Elena reads from her memoirs to those who had accompanied her on the Little Stroll, the narrator contemplates the difference between conversation and reading from a text.

While Elena is reading, "her eyes keep roaming over us. She spots every sign of boredom, every smile, every trace of indignation, and she'd like to respond, go into that point a bit more, shape it and serve it up in the most attractive way, but she can't. She's chained to that text, which was composed long ago, in solitude, for a different audience or, if for the same, one in a different mood" (72). The narrator, by contrast, favors conversation: "Ordinarily, despite the fact that people watch their words as closely as possible, conversation dips and flows, presses in one direction like ectoplasm, retreats, seeps onward: inexact, experimental, an amoeba possessing mobility but sluggish and perfectly adjustable to the lay of the land" (72). But ectoplasmic conversation, like the novel itself, threatens to lead nowhere but the narcissistic fantasy of the conclusion of the novel, into the imagination that one is a prince of the realm when, perhaps, one is nothing more than an irresponsible, masturbating boy.

Forgetting Elena reflects both the anxiety about and joy attendant on the brave new world promised by the many (including gay and lesbian) liberation movements that came to prominence in the 1960s, when the novel was written. It is a paranoid text that obscures its specifically gay content even as it celebrates the freedom from past sexual structures that were being promised by gay liberationists in the period. Nevertheless its refusal to settle questions about the self around gay identities makes it something of a queer work, as it once again anticipates social ideas that would come to prominence only two decades later, in the 1990s. The novel does not so much elaborate a gay identity or community as celebrate the freedom from traditional moral norms that makes a new order possible. If it worries about the narcissistic self-involvement of this new order, the novel also suggests there is no turning back. It ends, after all, with an Arrival.

Nocturnes for the King of Naples

As its title suggests, *Nocturnes for the King of Naples* is less topical than perhaps any other work by Edmund White. Even if its plot is a fantasy based on White's love for the actor Keith McDermott, the novel is a highly self-referential work of art. *Nocturne* is a musical term used to describe an often melancholic and moody type of music popularized in the nineteenth century, with Frédéric Chopin's nocturnes for piano being perhaps the most famous examples. White seems to use the term to suggest that, just as music can be a purely aesthetic "form," so, too, the novel may make its most compelling claims on the reader's imagination in formal ways. That speculation is perhaps borne out by the title's reference to the "King of Naples." Such a historical figure existed—at least through the Napoleonic period in Europe—but this is not a historical work, and no king literally appears in it. Indeed, it seems entirely possible White chose the phrase simply because it creates an intriguing (and beautiful) alliterative reversal of the "n" and "k" (or hard "c") sounds in *nocturnes*.

Nocturnes is not so much a traditionally structured novel as a series of prose poems or linguistic nocturnes on the theme of lost love. Directly addressing a lover rejected and then lost to death, an enigmatic "you" through whom the narrator explores metaphorically a number of abstract ideas about desire, it reveals its narrator, its speaking "I," in his effort to understand himself in relation to another, "you." Thus the structure of the entire novel recalls that brief moment in *Forgetting Elena* when the narrator misrecognized Herbert as a mirror image of himself. In the earlier novel, the narrator's self or identity seemed to come into being in the space of his difference from Herbert, and out of the emptiness of that space, he had to perceive and invent a way to understand himself. In *Nocturnes*, the narrator examines himself in the mirror of his memories of a lover he has left and who, we come to learn, has died before the young narrator can confess his love and atone for the sin of leaving. So, rather than discover a sense of self, he dwindles into a "ghost," a being lacking substance and life.[18]

The ideas about the narrator that emerge in *Nocturnes* are elaborated philosophically, as in the earlier novel, but also less abstractly, as White examines specifically the effects of sexuality and homosexuality on the narrator's person and self. On the one hand, White thinks of the self as an empty space of possibility, even a lack. It comes into being in relation to others and the social world one inhabits. Indeed, the profoundly pessimistic tone of *Nocturnes* derives in large part from its narrator's failure ever to locate himself within a social world offered by his former lover, hence his failure to locate a self at all. On the other hand, White seems specifically concerned with how this notion of the social self works itself out for a young gay man when dominant social models will not serve, when he, tragically, cannot yet accept the love offered him by another man. In *Nocturnes*, the young protagonist doesn't succeed even in the limited ways of the narrator of *Forgetting Elena*, perhaps because White explores, for the first time in his published fiction, issues he takes to be specific to gay life. For all its philosophical and aesthetic abstraction, *Nocturnes for the King of Naples* has something in common with the more socially realistic *A Boy's Own Story* in its exploration of a damaged gay psyche. Both reflect an experience of homosexuality as "tragic."[19]

The narrator of *Nocturnes* has grown up in a broken home. His father is immensely rich but unable to love anyone deeply or for long periods of time. His mother has been abandoned by his father and, at some point when the narrator is still an adolescent, kills herself. The narrator is raised in boarding schools, and by the time he reunites socially with his father, the older man is deep into an addiction to heroin and close to his death. His father seems unable to nurture and guide his teenaged son into adulthood, and, in fact, seems instead to develop an incestuous if not explicitly sexual dependence on him. It is at this point, as David Bergman notes, that the narrator meets his older lover, a man who becomes a "surrogate" for the father but who never succeeds in saving him from the damage already done to him by his family.[20] The novel is, then, primarily a study of character. It is about a boy so damaged by his family that he cannot escape it. When offered love, and an escape from his father, he ends up becoming like his father, unable to love deeply.

As one of the early gay novels published in America, *Nocturnes* reflects the lack of positive myths for gay people to live by when White was first writing.[21] In this sense, it perhaps helps us retrospectively to understand *Forgetting Elena,* which is concerned with its young narrator's emergence into a society so new that there are no myths at all by which to guide his living. One chapter of *Nocturnes* concerns the narrator's relationship with a young man he meets after leaving his older lover. Craig is an actor, and the two men make their home in an empty theater. In that setting, Craig and the narrator are able to create new and different "scenes" every night in which to explore their love and love-making. The suggestion is almost that the narrator seeks a script for his life as a lover and, perhaps, as a gay man. As it turns out, however, far from helping one another, both men fail at finding their proper role in relation to the other. Craig, the narrator reports, "had a beautiful indifference to human attachments, longings, jealousies, all of which he considered 'sticky'" (67), and the narrator, seeking to forget his former lover, "yearn[s] to imitate" Craig (68). But, ironically, it is Craig who imitates the narrator, for a relationship with someone indifferent to human attachments is bound not to last, and the narrator "fail[s] to work out" for Craig (74)—just as the narrator's lover failed to work out for him.

The novel examines what the narrator calls the "hydraulics of passion" (74), that is, the ways in which the two men's physical desires interact within a dynamic of emotion and individual self-assertion or power: "We love to give help but only to those who have no need of it, or more properly to those who desperately need it but proudly or despairingly refuse to accept it. We reach toward unreachable men in distress and toward no others. Self-sufficiency may inspire admiration but not love; frank, hungry need excites pity but tranquilizes desire" (73–74). The narrator's words speak as much about him as they do Craig. Both seem able to love only those who do not need them, which seems to rule everyone out in the pursuit of love—the narrator, who needs Craig, and his former lover, "you," who needs him. Whether this dynamic of power, need, and desire is to be understood as universal (the narrator speaks nebulously of "we," after all), whether it pertains to male sexual relations only, or whether it further characterizes the narrator's particular psychological condition is intriguing and debatable. Certainly it signals a longstanding thesis in White's work, one that we saw played out in *A Boy's Own Story* and *The Beautiful Room Is Empty,* and one that continues to hold the author's interest late into his career: the ways adult, gay desire can be structured in terms of power, mastery, and debasement when societies and individuals are unable to conceive it in more productive ways.

In *Nocturnes,* however, this power dynamic is also played out in a metaphysical key that brings the discussion of gay sex into relation with larger questions about the value and spiritual nature of love. The novel is infused with a religious imagery that, because it is simultaneously ironic and serious, is not easily understood. For example, one night toward the end of their relationship Craig and the narrator stage a scene that might have come from Shakespeare's *A Midsummer Night's Dream.* In "a misty forest" where "paper flowers are strewn across the floor and the ogival shadow of leaves play across our moving hands," Craig leads the narrator to "a secret bower canopied with luscious woodbine, sweet musk roses and eglantine"—the very words Oberon uses to describe Titania's bower in Shakespeare's play (79). Craig "places an animal's head over" the narrator's, "sheds his clothes until he is as smooth and pale as melting candlewax," and then dons "cellophane wings stretched over veins of wire" (79–80). In this likeness of a fairy, Craig woos the bestial narrator, exciting in him "the lust of a true lover," who in seeking to possess his lover's body longs to own his "*soul*" (80). But while such metaphysical posturing produces an ecstatic vision of love, we might nevertheless remain skeptical. Rather than reveal a genuine transcendence, the narrator's coupling with the godlike Craig only suggests to him an "inevitable sense of unworthiness" that intensifies as the lovers transform themselves even more fully into an allegory of bestial flesh in its encounter with the divine (80). Godlike, Craig presents himself as an object of worship and adoration that assumes fleshly form to make love to the animal the narrator has become. In the small scene (which, again, stages an idea not entirely alien to Shakespeare's play) the lust-inducing, naked Craig represents himself as "a power that can never be seen" but one that nevertheless "is in fact here, seen and seeing" (81).

Craig, posing as a god, characteristically reveals himself to be more involved with his own self than with the narrator, an idea White wittily reveals through an oblique reference to the myth of Narcissus and Echo. In making love to the narrator, Craig is only "an echo to his own shout" (82). So, the scene almost seems to parody Craig's narcissism, and rightly so. But it critiques as well the narrator, whose relationship to Craig is a compound of unworthy admiration, godlike love, and emotional indifference that leads nowhere. It is only one of several moments in the novel when the narrator characterizes the object of his or other men's lust or desire as godlike in a way White characterizes as both narcissistic and self-defeating. The conflation of body and soul represented in the scene is not genuine but the product of costume, scenery, and self-absorption. Despite his love (and lust) for Craig, the narrator recognizes that this is an "act," and that he does not have the "fortitude to proceed, step by delicious and aching step, through an act" (81).

These scenes with Craig provide an important clue to the meaning of the novel as a whole. Craig's sterile narcissism contrasts the more genuine love of the narrator's rejected lover, the novel's unseen "you." In his relationship to Craig the narrator plays out a sexual dynamic in which he seeks a love he characterizes as godlike but that stands in place of and in some ways precludes the honest emotional attachment he found with his lover. It is a dynamic he seems doomed to repeat over and over. At the opening of the novel, for instance, the narrator has already left his lover and is cruising for sex on ruined piers like the ones that used to line the Hudson River in Manhattan. The scene boldly and explicitly reveals the rituals of gay promiscuity at the time, and it may have seemed deliberately shocking when White compared the decaying piers to a "ruined cathedral" (1) and gay men's cruising to "their search for [a] god" (5). Nevertheless, the passage brilliantly characterizes the narrator's obsessive and ultimately fruitless search for an ecstatic sexual connection and a seeming god to replace his older, lost lover.

The haunting imagery of the narrator's wandering through religious monuments in ruin equates his present loveless condition with a loss of faith, and it expresses a sense that his present life is somehow a penalty for his failing to recognize real love when it was offered to him. We learn toward the end of the book that this moment occurs shortly after the narrator's breakup with his lover. So, everything that happens to him subsequently—that is, everything recorded in the novel—seems to be part of his punishment. White reinforces the point late in the story, when the narrator is returning from a visit with his former lover's friends. He looks around him on the boat he travels on and says, "As I looked at the other passengers, I could easily pick out those expressionless, intriguing beauties I address as *you*, those same faces, dark or fair, brooding or elated, whom I'd always believed I could love, even if I'd seen them only for a moment on a train or a bus or passing me on the street as I headed away from your dinner table" (148). The sad detail is that the "you" who initially had been so real, so physically embodied that he is remembered at his dinner table, becomes anyone the narrator imagines can stand in as the substitute object of love and desire. Having rejected a lover who, like a real god, returned his love, the narrator can now only play his love out among the myriad reflections of a lost original.

J. D. McClatchy suggests that the novel represents "the Psyche's reminiscence of Eros, and its chapters are the narrator's meditations on the echoes of an original erotic transcendence in his subsequent affairs and ménages, which comprise the world of experience fallen from a mysterious grace."[22] The point is obviously relevant to the narrator's sad, obsessive search for a replacement for his lost lover. Taken in context of the whole novel, the narrator's search for "god" seems to be an expression of regret for a life in which he has come to resemble the walking dead. The narrator refers to himself as a "an unenthusiastic Lazarus . . . coaxed up out of the grave" (123), which implies that, even though the novel itself is a record of his thoughts and memories, his life and his body have withered into nothingness through his devotion to an idea of his former lover who is now beyond recovery. Toward the end, the narrator writes, "moralists say that our actions and not our intentions define us, and by that harsh rule I lose all definition" (133). He is, finally, a man willing to judge himself harshly by what he has done or failed to do in the world, and not by what he intended to do. That may be his best, most admirable quality.

But the metaphysics of eroticism McClatchy discerns in the novel can also be interpreted in other ways. In the first place, the imagery that equates an elusive object of desire with a god also attaches itself to the narrator's former lover, who is referred to late in the novel as "a man or god who has died"

(147). In this sense, the novel literally becomes, as Neil Bartlett points out, "a piece of devotional literature dedicated to a dead lover."[23] The narrator's leaving his lover seems to be a type of apostasy that he has to confess and atone for by writing the novel itself. Speaking about how he tries to evade the implications of his life, the narrator writes that "best of all [the] agents of dilution is fiction—either the fiction of memory or fantasy—for it alone dissolves the entire scene in the cloud, brilliant or black, of desire" (124). He therefore produces his series of nocturnes, all addressed to "you," a figure who is, on one level, a character remembered in the novel but who is, on another level, something more abstract, the lover who now comes to seem godlike only—and too late—in the abstract terms of fiction and memory.

If, however, *Nocturnes* seems to judge its narrator by implying that he comes to see his former lover as godlike only once he is gone, it also suggests that his imagining love in such metaphysical terms may all along have been the problem. White is always aware in his novels of the difficulties that arise when love and simple desire are made to bear too much metaphysical weight, and not valued for themselves. As we saw in the descriptions of the narrator's sex with Craig, White produces a lush erotic prose in *Nocturnes*, one that echoes the erotic obsession and stylistic excess of classical baroque literature and art. The implication of such baroque art has always been that desire marks a path toward spiritual ecstasy. But the narrator's inability to take the love offered him by his unnamed lover on its own human terms reflects and inspires a self-absorption that White explores as the underside of such over-determined eroticism.

The narrator says that his "longing to get away" from his lover seemed "almost metaphysical" to him (14). His words imply he rejects his original lover, the mysterious "you," because he longs for an erotic transcendence that cannot be satisfied by his (the lover's) simple self-sufficiency, a quality, we heard the narrator say earlier, that inspires "admiration," not "love" (74). White suggests, then, that the narrator's search for a god not only post-dates but predates their split. It is not the result but the origin of his bad faith in love. The peculiar "hydraulics of passion" the novel explores are ones in which the narrator detaches sexual desire from bodies that exist independently of his fantasies, so that love for him becomes primarily a sterile, narcissistic pleasure, like that he experienced with Craig (74). It is only once his rejected lover is dead—can make no demands and return no love—that the narrator sees that the real-life love he offered was a superior kind of divinity. Only when he can distance himself from desire by translating it into art, the writing of the "devotional" novel itself, does the narrator come to feel it profoundly. So, even his devotion and contrition seem self-serving.

The point is made vividly when, at the opening of chapter 4, the narrator invokes Gregory of Nyssa's exegetical method in interpreting the Song of Songs. Although he accuses this man of the church of privately savoring the eroticism of the biblical story, he also says that Gregory uses words to expunge one set of meanings (sexual ones) in favor of others (spiritual ones). It is the narrator's method as well. He, too, engages a certain masturbatory relish in his writing even as he adopts the exegete's self-serving manner when he interprets his own words.[24] "For I, too," he writes, "will relish an amorous history, then lift a hand from the page or my pleasure and find in vivid scenes portents" (43). He attempts to shape his memories into something more seemingly substantive than erotic in an impossible effort to charm a lover beyond his reach: "I simply want to anticipate your laughter at *my* method, which will be his" (43). That, however, his dead lover can respond to him is only a pleasant and narcissistic illusion. His writing serves—and pleases—only himself. Thus we might understand one of the mysteries of the narrator's address to "you." If, in writing, "I" create the "you" that reflects back onto me, then I have never left myself at all. His writing of the novel itself reflects the same narcissistic self-absorption that led the narrator to reject his lover in the first place.

Indeed, this point brings us to one of the great difficulties in understanding *Nocturnes*, its address to a character who appears primarily in the second person as "you." Although the "you" of White's novel stands most concretely for the narrator's lost lover, and we can understand the novel by accepting this simple identification, it represents as well a number of other ideas, including some abstractions. "You" also seems easily to stand for the reader who may or may not exhibit sympathy for the narrator. It stands for the many individual gods the narrator appeals to for love (as we've seen), and it may stand for some genuine god, to whom the narrator implicitly appeals for absolution. "You" even seems to be other aspects of the narrator's self—especially his past self—who sit in judgment on the person he has become.[25] In appealing to any or all of these figures embodied only as "you," the narrator attempts to control and shape their perception of him, to show contrition, and to seek forgiveness—no matter how hopeless the task may ultimately seem in light of the power of the novel's many readers or perceivers, its many evocations of "you," to withhold sympathy, love, and understanding. However we read this evocative figure, "you" is someone to whom the narrator must appeal for an absolution he seems unwilling to afford himself. The device makes clear that the narrator's writing the novel is not simply an act of devotion and contrition, but a simultaneous confession that provides scant hope for forgiveness.

White is always noteworthy as a stylist, and in *Nocturnes* the style achieves prominence as the medium of his protagonist's narcissistic evocation of self. The narrator's writing a series of extraordinarily complex and beautiful poems addressed outward, to some unknown, "you," represents the production of a lyric "I," who speaks himself into being by rendering his memories in terms of great beauty. The novel is literally a meta-fiction in the sense that it concerns the narrator's effort to write the implications of his life into a form of art. If, however, his confession to his many readers suggests he is seeking to redeem an authentic self lost when he rejected his lover, the novel's evocation of that self only in the play of language that exists between an "I" who speaks and a "you" who perceives suggests the impossibility of such an act.

Unlike White's later autobiographical novels, in which the voice of the narrator calls into being a gay character otherwise not represented in American society, here the narrator's voice seems only to echo what has come before and what has been lost to him. This narrator cannot embrace the possibilities of self-invention, the "mysterious invitations to happiness or pain" that "must be called 'You'" (147). Acknowledging to his rejected lover that "the old law was being lifted by you, word by word, the prohibitions broken" (146), the narrator nevertheless pursued and continues to pursue the "'I's' that speak to [his own] experience" (147), and finds himself trapped there. If he writes himself into being, his language and words merely record a self that might have been. In this respect, *Nocturnes* may seem to glance at the social world of 1970s America, serving as a gloomy riposte to those who failed to take full account and advantage of the changes coming about all around them.

Caracole

White began, although he did not finish, *Caracole* before he wrote and published *A Boy's Own Story*. But despite appearing chronologically after his most famous autobiographical work, the style and theme of the novel link it to *Forgetting Elena* and *Nocturnes for the King of Naples*. *Caracole* looks closely at the social and political impotence of the highly intellectualized societies that seem to have fascinated White at this period, and its trenchant critique of the rarefied social and intellectual milieu it describes perhaps makes clearer White's ambivalence about the New Code being forged by Herbert in *Forgetting Elena*. The world described there and in *Caracole* is rich with possibility for someone open to novelty and able to live outside the cloying structures of traditional morality. But its pleasures and possibilities do not necessarily sustain human emotional connections in their richest variety. Like his other novels, then, *Caracole* reveals the characteristic that makes White's analysis of the emergence of America's sexual subcultures so valuable: its clear-headed insight into what is lost and gained in the new worlds of sexual freedom of the 1960s and 1970s.

What is perhaps most intriguing about *Caracole* is that it entirely lacks gay content, a fact that created difficulties for White's gay readers when the novel was first published. If we understand that period as a time when gay men had difficulty finding literature that reflected their own experiences, we might understand their disappointment. Perhaps ironically (because White's sexuality is so public), the novel's lack of gay content is due in part to its origins in autobiography. *Caracole* fictionalizes the story of White's late nephew Keith Fleming, who came to live in New York with White in January 1976. Fleming had a troubled adolescence following the divorce of his mother, White's sister Margaret, from her husband. Keith's father eventually had the boy confined to a psychiatric institution, and Margaret sought White's help in getting him out.[26]

Keith lived with his uncle for nearly a year, and his arrival in New York was soon followed by that of his friend Laura, a young Mexican-American girl that Keith had met in one of the psychiatric facilities his father had placed him in. These events created a situation highly unusual for the time, one in which the openly gay White became, in effect, the guardian of his adolescent nephew. They also provided White an occasion for exploring a situation similar to that of *Forgetting Elena,* one in which a young man comes to maturity in a sophisticated and highly refined world, only this time it is clearly heterosexuality that White explores through his young protagonist. So, we should not overlook the importance of *Caracole* in the continuing development of White's ideas about sexuality, especially its implication that the eruption of adolescent sexuality into a troubling world of mature experience is not simply a gay story.

It is, however, a story that might be understood differently from a "gay perspective," as the English writer Neil Bartlett claims when he argues that *Caracole* is not a gay text in the sense that it is a "text 'about' gayness" but rather one in which White makes the assumption that "a gay version of the world might be a true one."[27] What that version fully entails is a matter for debate, but the novel's insistence that sex is integral and fundamental to mature living is surely one aspect of that perspective, as is, perhaps, its refusal of the sentimental notion that adolescence belongs to the realm of childhood innocence from sex rather than adult experience of it. *Caracole* also measures intellect and morality against the body as a source of desire. Although it doesn't confuse the pleasures of the physical with the demands of intellect, it also refuses to undervalue them. If the novel suggests that desire cannot be fully intellectualized, it nevertheless suggests that its effects, pursued rightly, provide a salutary gloss to humane thought and civil living. It was not only gay thinkers in the 1970s and 1980s who believed such things, but such thinking was integral to the development of gay thought.

Caracole is set largely in an unnamed, mythically evoked capital city that could be Paris under the Nazi occupation or nineteenth-century Rio under the Portuguese, although it most nearly resembles Venice under the domination of the Austrian Hapsburgs in the nineteenth century. That it reflects White's life in 1970s Manhattan as well makes apparent the semi-allegorical nature of the setting, in which White once again takes up the relationship he had explored in *Forgetting Elena* between older social orders and newer ones. In this case, White examines the tensions among the conquerors who have recently come to dominate the country, the intellectuals whose relationship to these conquerors is highly complex and ambiguous, and those native populations and long-established families associated with the land itself. These last groups have an ambiguous relationship both to the ruling and the intellectual elite, but White associates them with a more natural embodiment of sex and desire than is to be found in the capital. Not surprisingly, it is someone from this group, the young protagonist Gabriel, who becomes the symbol of social and political resistance to the conquering regime and who will become the leader of a revolution at the end of the novel. These developments suggest that White is not interested in political insurrection *per se* but the revolution in ideas about sexuality and intellect emerging in the late 1970s when the novel was initially drafted.

The novel's allegorical dimensions are highlighted in the first chapter, which serves as a prologue and takes place outside the city, in a jungle-like setting. The protagonist, Gabriel, is a boy from an important, landed family whose fortunes have decayed. Because his mother's ill health confines her to bed, where she grows grotesquely fat and immobile, he is free to spend most of his days roaming unsupervised through the jungle landscape where he lives. When Gabriel meets a native girl, Angelica, he falls in love and discovers sex. Although he marries Angelica in a native ceremony, his father, who has been largely absent in his life, reappears and imprisons him in a dark cage. There is a suggestion that Gabriel's transgression of ethnic boundaries in his love for Angelica disturbs Gabriel's father, but White seems more interested in exploring the emergence of sexual desire in his young protagonist and the effects of Gabriel's father's crossing that desire. During the time Gabriel is imprisoned, "sleeping and masturbating were his two pleasures," though he "preferred fantasies to dreams because he could steer fantasies, refine them, continue them."[28] Thus White quietly introduces what will become the dominant themes of his novel: sex, desire, and power, both personal and political or social power, and the role of sex in creating productive social selves. Gabriel is rescued from his imprisonment and from the forces of sexual repression represented by his father only when his Uncle Mateo arrives from the capital of the province and takes the boy home to live with him.

The early part of the novel, then, begins as fairy tale. Its jungle landscape peopled with mysterious natives is both sexually and politically charged: it suggests the labyrinthine situation of the sexual unconscious that lies behind any young person's coming of age in civil society, and White links Gabriel's escape from a personally and sexually oppressive social world to the struggle for independence from the ruling regime that dominates the capital to which Mateo takes the boy. The mythical landscape of Gabriel's ancestral home echoes novels written in the tradition (associated often with South American writers) of magical realism in which fantastic eruptions into more mundane reality suggest the politicized memories of a land and its people. In *Caracole*, this mythic environment points toward the memory of those aspects of desire and bodily freedom that are perverted in the overly refined response of the capital's intellectual elite to its conquering force. One might imagine that such revolution as the novel promises will integrate love and desire with social and political integrity in ways Gabriel and the other characters in the novel have not so far experienced.

One of the difficulties of *Caracole* is that Gabriel's maturation does not develop in a linear fashion. For the first time in his published novels, White writes in the third-person point of view, a decision that increases his capacity for commenting on the inner lives of a multitude of characters. Nevertheless the novel's abrupt shifts and abundant commentary create for the reader something of the dazzling confusion Gabriel himself feels once he leaves the jungle—not always with happy effect. Still, the novel's complexity seems easier to grasp if we recognize that Gabriel's maturation unfolds around three triangular relationships that involve him either directly or indirectly and intersect with one another over the course of the whole. In one, Gabriel himself has an affair with the much older Mathilda, who is the friend and former lover of Mateo (the father, we come to learn, of her son, Daniel). In the second triangle, Gabriel has an affair with Edwige, the woman loved by his Uncle Mateo but who does not love him back. And in the third, Mateo finds himself in a sexual relationship with Angelica, Gabriel's "wife" who has come to live in the capital and become financially dependent on Mateo. The structural complexity of the novel keeps the focus on Gabriel and his relationship with his uncle and Angelica, even when any one of the three becomes only tangential to the action. More important, it provides White an extraordinarily flexible structure for exploring his most important theme: adult sexual power and experience, and the ways Gabriel and Angelica come to understand and master them.

The first significant romantic triangle of the novel details both how Gabriel comes to understand the power of his body and sex as well as the ways love softens (at least initially) the overly intellectual Mathilda. If *Caracole* is a bildungsroman, a novel about the education and maturation of Gabriel, it is more precisely a novel of sexual education. Gabriel not only listens to his uncle expostulate on love and desire, but he learns himself how to control their energies. So, by the end of the novel, when he inevitably reunites with Angelica, and takes his place as the symbolic leader of a revolution, we might be somewhat confident that the new order Gabriel will lead is a more carefully integrated world of intellect and desire than the present one. Gabriel's sexual education, which is not incompatible with his more general education, begins when he first meets Mathilda and realizes that the natural, unsophisticated sex he had experienced in the jungle with Angelica can be exploited in more sophisticated ways in the city.

For one thing, he comes to understand that sex is a currency that can be manipulated in the exchange of social power and advantage. So, for instance, when Mathilda challenges Gabriel's assertion that he comes from an "unusual family" she manifests what the novel elsewhere refers to as a rather insincere intellectual habit of challenging whatever people say (whether she agrees or not) and pretending to comprehend their point more fully than they do. "So do we all. Monster parents, bourgeois hypocrisy, provincial views—I see it all and nothing could be more banal" (73). But rather than putting her off, Gabriel's angry defiance of her intellectual pretension—"I don't think you quite grasp the originality of my situation" (73)—intrigues Mathilda. Gabriel comes to recognize "that only a measure of independence was likely to attract her; he must insist *she* please *him*" (74), and he sees in Mathilda's eyes "the same sequence of desire that would twitch jerkily through Angelica's" (74–75). The scene ends with both Gabriel and Mathilda watching "the blue silk pleat of [Gabriel's] pants stretch and fill" (75).

Gabriel learns that even intellectuals respond to the excitation of physical desire properly negotiated. When he attends the first of Mathilda's soirees, composed of the most formidable and famous intellectuals in the city, he is so nervous about saying something wrong in reply to Mathilda's tirade against intellectuals (her friends and guests) that he says nothing. He just takes "her hand between his," which makes Mathilda shudder "with pleasure" (105).

It is a complicated scene in which Gabriel comprehends the ways of social flattery among the most brilliant in society. But he also learns that, even when one cannot contribute to the brilliant conversation, one can score points through the body: "No one was as smart as Mathilda, that was obvious. Luckily he had no points to make. By touching her, by putting their two bodies into contact, he'd shifted their exchange onto a more shadowy plain where she was less sure of herself" (106). Thus Gabriel comes to understand more fully the power of desire, and his own ability to exploit it.

White complicates the situation by implying that Gabriel's desire for Mathilda may proceed from little more than his feeling flattered by her, but for Mathilda the relationship comes to signify her need to understand what, as an intellectual, she has often neglected: her body, with its needs and desires separate from those of the intellect. Unfortunately she never seems to understand that Gabriel's youth, his physical prowess, provides him a power as potent as her own intellectual strength, one that she, with her middle-aged body, cannot replicate. So, while she attempts to maintain her hold on Gabriel with reference to her social and intellectual power, his interests turn toward the exquisitely beautiful Edwige, which produces another test for the boy.

In his elaboration of the relationship between Gabriel and Mateo's erst-while lover, Edwige, White explores fully the meaning and importance of physical desire, for not only is this relationship characterized through highly explicit representations of sex, but it is the one about which the narrator writes that "with Edwige [Gabriel] was in love for the first time; he loved Edwige and until now he had been incomplete" (277). The key ingredient it seems is Edwige's frank understanding that it is the body, consciously manipulated, that produces desire and the "feeling" of love (277). There are no obfuscations around intellect in her desire for Gabriel. Sex, she teaches him, is a means to attain pleasure, of all sorts. Mateo warns Gabriel about her: "She never pays for a ride, in a hired vehicle . . . or rather the payment never involves money" (273). But his unflattering revelation does not, appar-ently, deter Mateo himself, or his nephew. Describing Gabriel's first true sexual encounter with Edwige, White writes that "her very acquisitiveness in pursuing a specific sexual quest excited him, made him harder. . . . He was merely the perpetrator of their mutual pleasure" (268). Whereas Mathilda had taught Gabriel "the doctrine of love as salvation," he had "learned it without feeling it" (277).

The downside to the uses of the flesh that Edwige has so thoroughly mas-tered is that there is no center to hold it steady. Edwige wants to love Gabriel, but the emotional complexity of his love for her creates expectations she can't fulfill. She never learns what role she is supposed to play with Gabriel, and so consequently ends up betraying him and breaking his heart. Significantly, although his relationship with Edwige makes it apparent to Gabriel how "dowdy" was the "talkative and serious world of Mathilda's and Mateo's friends," he seems by this point to have developed a complexity of emotion far surpassing Edwige's (270). While she may seem to be the most sexually free of the capital's inhabitants, "Edwige had never been able to love wisely" (280). Indeed, by her own admission, she may even be "incapable of loving" (281). In this sense, she represses some dimension of erotic experience that seems to be promised for Gabriel when he reunites with Angelica.

In the third triangular relationship in the novel, the one between Angelica and Mateo, White suggests alternatives to the dysfunctions Gabriel encounters in his relationships with Mathilda and Edwige, and presumably the power of these alternatives will be translated to him when he reunites with Angelica at the end of the novel. Like Mathilda, Mateo is acutely aware that he has become middle-aged, but unlike her and more like Edwige, he seems to understand that sex can be a power for negotiation rather than a simple urge that overpowers. It is easy to read White's representation of the desire Angelica feels for Mateo as a middle-aged man's fantasy, and perhaps it is. But throughout his writing White seems interested in exploring the ways sex and desire produce power and enable transformations for people in unexpected ways—even young people. Although his primary focus seems to be on Mateo, White suggests that the beneficial consequences of his character's relationship to Angelica extend to her as well. In this case, it does so because Mateo grasps an idea that Mathilda, in her relationship to Gabriel, never does: middle-aged, indeed old, people engage in a balletic "adagio" with younger partners (126). The young may indulge "the disinterested father" who will "listen to their problems, fan their aspirations" (126). Certainly "the young assumed desire died by middle age except among the perverted few. They were disgusted by advances from their elders as though to cross the generations were a form of bestiality" (126).

Nevertheless Mateo recognizes that, when a young woman does give her favors to an older man, she helps him create "a new young face for himself" (126), and that if, in this exchange of intimacy "a girl . . . hope[s] to gain something from him . . . he could take comfort in the candor of her duplicity" (127). "A straightforward trade of influence for intimacy was worldly, fair, even (if seen in the right light) cheerful" (127). As Stephen Barber puts it, Mateo "experiences a kind of physical resuscitation through Angelica's body,"[29] and his response is gratitude: "Mateo detested middle-aged men (and women) who ceased to feel gratitude to their young lovers, who became so foolish as to imagine that youth and beauty *owe* sexual favors to age and experience" (294). If, however, Angelica's compensation for loving Mateo is partly material, the novel also suggests that it doesn't preclude love, for Angelica comes to love Mateo not for his looks but his kindness: "I fell in love with you because of your kindness, because I like myself when I'm with you, because you see everything about me and still like me, because I have the feeling you need me and no one ever needed me before . . ." (295). Love in the novel is a complicated interplay of material need, mutual flattery, realistic self-appraisal, and, as we saw in the case of Gabriel and Mathilda, sheer bluff. In their interactions with older lovers, both Gabriel and Angelica come to master it.

Although we have been looking at the relationships that structure *Caracole* in terms of couples, there is always a third partner in these relationships. White keeps a focus either on Mateo (in Gabriel's relationships to Mathilda and Edwige) or Gabriel (in Mateo's relationship to Angelica). He thus keeps the reader's attention on the novel's most important relationship, the one between Gabriel and his uncle, and emphasizes the ways Gabriel comes to supplant his uncle in power and influence. Mateo and Gabriel come from a family whose power to serve as a symbol for revolutionary realignment in the kingdom has been assumed throughout. But it is Gabriel and not Mateo who ultimately seems poised to fulfill that promise. In part, it has to do with his youth and sexual potency. *Caracole* is less clearly about genuine political insurrection than power and sexual knowledge. In fact, the novel provides very little knowledge of the political events taking place in its background, but the imagination of potency, sexual and otherwise, reflect metonymically the power that brings about change, and it is Gabriel who is the most potent character in the novel. What he brings to the capital is not political knowledge but instinctual sexual power that becomes refined during his educational process. Readers who were initially inclined to dismiss the novel as something of a retreat from White's concern with homosexuality miss the ways in which it is about the power of sexuality in general as a social phenomenon and force—an idea directly relevant to thinking about gay social relations in 1970s and 1980s America.

The emphasis on the relationship between Gabriel and Mateo also gives specific focus to the novel's social satire. No small part of the delight in reading *Caracole* derives from White's skewering the pretensions of the intellectual society to which Mateo belongs. There is no doubt that Mathilda's circle represents the most brilliant public face of intellectual life in the capital (a face that explicitly reflects the intellectual life of Manhattan during the 1970s), for Mateo tells Gabriel that "commerce, law, philosophy, history itself got shaped by this lot" (117). But the novel calls into question their claims to continuing political power and social relevance—especially in their inability to negotiate the brave new sexual and political world emerging around them. The novel reveals its intellectuals not only as self-serving, but impotent, and because they are impotent, malicious: "Their impotence made them irritable" (78).

Perhaps it is precisely this point we see illustrated in the trajectory of Mathilda's relationship with Gabriel. We've already seen something of Mathilda's insecurity in this love affair, but as the novel progresses we understand more fully her sexual and political irrelevance. While Mathilda's faction opposes the current conquering regime, and while her actions help usher in the revolution promised at the end of the novel, it is not because of any conscious political decision Mathilda makes. Rather, it is because her jealous despair leads her to shoot and kill Edwige at the most important costume ball in the city. Her action disrupts an important civic occasion, providing a symbolic focus for the revolution that has already been fomented among the local citizens, and creates the occasion for Gabriel to assume his role as leader. But it proceeds from her extraordinarily misguided sense of identification with and patronizing understanding of the very people whose political interests she presumes to support: "primitives," she thinks, "did things—attacked, killed, struck back—and sobered up later to regret their impetuosity. Civilized people did nothing and prided themselves on the self-consciousness that had tranquilized them" (327). Mathilda's actions, ironically, reveal that she is neither "primitive" nor "civilized," for although she acts, she remains tranquilized to all but her own personal animosities and interests.

The extent to which Mateo and Mathilda's world has failed them is made clear in a touching, and oddly romantic, moment toward the end of the novel when it becomes clear that these two have missed the opportunities that await Gabriel and Angelica—both romantic opportunities and the opportunity to make a positive impact on future change. Mathilda comes to Mateo in her grief over Gabriel's betrayal. While the scene reflects brilliantly the rich complexity of a longstanding friendship, it expresses something as well of a regret, at least on the part of Mateo, that he had not discovered with and for Mathilda the kind of love he has experienced with Angelica. Clearly they were in love in the past, as might be inferred by the news Mathilda reveals that Daniel is their son. But at this point (doomed perhaps to their cynicism) Mateo cannot express simple human sympathy for Mathilda, and she can only vex him by revealing the news that Gabriel has left her for Mateo's former love, Edwige. So while *Caracole* as a whole creates a sense of change in the society it describes, that change is not being fostered by intellectuals and artists such as Mateo. Change appears from the ground up, and is symbolized by Mateo's primary competitor, the increasingly virile Gabriel.

For Gabriel and Angelica, the end of the novel promises something better. In the concluding pages, they are re-united at, presumably, just the right time, after they have both learned to master their bodies and pleasures within the sophisticated, intellectual world of the novel. They literally gain experience over the course of the novel that can be usefully contrasted to their condition at the outset, when their natural passion reflected clumsy unfocused bodily desire alone. This is a key point. The success of Gabriel and Angelica's love does not depend upon their innocence but the complexity and nuance provided by their "fall" into experience. It is this idea, perhaps, that explains one of the most difficult aspects of *Caracole*, White's flirtation with the forbidden fruit of adolescent-adult relationships. If White's representation of intergenerational sexual relationships seems shocking in twenty-first century America, his excuse may be that he understands the body as a source of pleasure and pain, an impediment but also a conduit to love one has to learn through experience to control. As we saw in *A Boy's Own Story,* White's adolescents are fully sentient sexual beings, and they cannot master either their sexuality or their maturation outside the signifying practices of adult experience. White might be accused of romanticizing intergenerational love by representing it outside the exploitative possibilities that potentially structure such relations. But he seems willing to risk that criticism to demonstrate the efficacy of his characters' yoking youthful power to adult knowledge. Experience for White is "not a question of losing innocence [but] . . . of gaining in cunning."[30]

Caracole is not naïve about what adult love and knowledge means, the guilt it draws on, the obligations it entails, and the power it provides those who understand it. In a complicated passage, White shows that Mateo understands that his power over Gabriel and Angelica derives "from his forbearance," his strategy of not confronting their ignorance or guile with open resistance. Consequently Gabriel believes that he is "gaining a soul" from his uncle's constant, gentle questioning. But if the narrator wryly suggests that, instead, Gabriel is "being instilled with guilt," Mateo reconstructs his sense of time and place in the world: "At Madder Pink he'd awakened every morning with no regrets for yesterday and no fear of tomorrow; no wonder his sense of time remained rudimentary. But in the capital . . . Gabriel [learned] to scan everything he and other people said or did for clues. Experience was no longer an engulfing wave but an elaborate meal whose recipe must be reconstructed by guesswork" (213–14).

Experience, that condition the hapless narrators of *Forgetting Elena* and *Nocturnes for the King of Naples* avoid in their flights from adult knowledge, provides a continuity of understanding, knowledge of one's place in larger systems such as time and family that connect one to other people, no matter how vexing that connection might be. This explains, perhaps, how Gabriel's role in leading the incipient revolution at the end of the novel signals a kind of maturity, for in taking up his own family's traditional place as leaders among these now conquered people, he merges past, present, and future into a coherent whole: "With the simplifying grandeur of destiny, [Angelica] knelt beside Gabriel and began to explain to him what he must do and who he'd become" (342). Although Barber rightly notes that "the unique rôle which is ultimately assigned . . . Gabriel . . . parallels the assumption by the narrator of *Forgetting Elena* of his special responsibility,"[31] here one has, perhaps, more confidence in Gabriel's ability to act to transform not simply himself but his world.

CHAPTER FIVE

Historical Novels

Fanny: A Fiction and Hotel de Dream: A New York Story

White's first two novels of the twenty-first century, *Fanny: A Fiction* and *Hotel de Dream: A New York Novel,* take a new and seemingly unexpected turn into history—although by now we should not be surprised by the many experiments coming from the pen of the writer literary historian Gregory Woods has aptly dubbed "the most interesting, adventurous and ambitious of the American gay novelists."[1] White himself has explained his turn to the historical "partly" as a "flight from 'I.' In other words, you know, if you're writing so much stuff about yourself, you get fed up with that and you want to . . . enact your own dramas in other terms."[2] Even so, as early as the short story "An Oracle," White was looking toward ancient Greece to create an "analogue" for understanding modern homosexual relations,[3] and his return to a specifically American history no doubt reflects a similar desire to understand himself and contemporary history through the past. White was not alone in turning to history as a way of thinking about sexuality and homosexuality at the turn of the twenty-first century, for other gay writers such as David Leavitt—in several short stories as well as *While England Sleeps* (1993) and *The Indian Clerk* (2007)—and Colm Tóibín—in *The Master* (2004)—had also returned to earlier periods in Anglo-American literature and life to reveal something about the ways sexuality is and is not the same in different historical moments.

The groundbreaking work of thinkers such as Michel Foucault and Jeffrey Weeks makes clear that there is a history of sex. Sexuality and hence homosexuality are always constituted in historically specific ways, and our efforts to think about them in the past are prone to distortion if we impose what Robert D. Fulk calls an "ethnocentric modern view on all of history."[4] Even though White himself has been the great chronicler of particular formulations of sexual identity in America at the end of the twentieth century, he has also been acutely aware, in Tony Purvis's words, that there are "no typical Americans, gays, or gay Americans."[5] We should not be surprised then to find him returning to history to understand something about the ways sexual behaviors were enacted differently in earlier periods. White's (and other gay writers') historical novels represent an effort to understand sexual difference in other times and places and to create, in Fulk's word, an analogue for understanding the present. For White in particular, the emphasis is on social critique. Both *Fanny* and *Hotel de Dream* are concerned with how and why American history and culture have effaced radically alternative sexualities and the ways writing allows us to recover them. The novels mark a double effacement: the first one committed by history, as it erases sexual Others, and the second one committed on history, as White gives voice to otherwise erased sexual lives and stories.

Fanny

A historical novel about two fiercely independent nineteenth-century women (the fiery Scottish reformer Frances (Fanny) Wright and the English popular novelist Frances (Fanny) Trollope) *Fanny: A Fiction* (2003) is, on the surface, a radical departure for White. Set in the nineteenth century, it necessarily eschews the personal, autobiographical narrative White is famous for writing, and for the most part is not about sexuality or homosexuality, White's most characteristic themes. White's conceit is that the novel itself is the manuscript of a biography of Frances Wright left unfinished by Frances Trollope when she died. Consequently White writes in the fully heterosexual, female voice of the nineteenth-century novelist rather than his own. But while the garrulous narrator, Trollope, purports to be writing about Wright, she cannot stop speaking about herself. So, White's fictionalized biography seems increasingly to become a fictionalized autobiography.

To complicate matters, by the end of the novel, the by-now very old Mrs. Trollope confesses to not knowing much about some key matters in Fanny Wright's life (her intimate relations with a series of powerful men, for instance), and she even seems to have trouble recalling what she is writing, at which point we might imagine she is creating exactly what the title of the novel claims itself to be, a fiction. Of course, the joke—coming as all this does from the pen of a master writer of biographies—depends on White's apprehension of how any biography, and indeed any autobiography, might very well prove to be little more than fanciful self-promotion. In *Fanny*, White seems to have a great deal of fun playing with questions of literary genre (questions that, incidentally, might be posed about his own writing): What is the difference between fiction and biography or autobiography? How much does a writer's ego misshape his or her apprehension of the subject?

And yet, for all its seeming difference from White's earlier works, *Fanny*, his eighth published novel, "maintains a clear connection to White's long-standing preoccupations."[6] Characteristically, White uses the multiple ambiguities and ironies of this "fiction" to raise questions about American social life and mores, especially as it comes into contact with European ones. Purvis links the novel to any number of White's earlier works in its effort to confront its reader "with the operations and ethics of power in America."[7] Equally to the point, White's emphasis on the uncertainties of its narrator's voice—which refer the novel as far back in White's oeuvre as *Forgetting Elena*—tends to destabilize our understanding of its critique and render both Fannys equally admirable and suspect. The novel is simultaneously a critique and celebration of a perhaps fatally flawed new world in America, for at its most fundamental level, *Fanny* is a historical fiction that allows White to juxtapose two ways of seeing and understanding the social experiment in democracy and living that took place in nineteenth-century America: one idealistic and attuned to the possibilities of the new, and another more fully aware of the debts and obligations of traditional familial or domestic values. Presumably the conclusions he draws are, as with any good historical fiction, of continuing relevance.

Both Fannys in White's novel are remarkably like their real-life counterparts. Frances Wright was the daughter of a prosperous Scottish merchant who was himself a free thinker and idealist. She was orphaned early, and left well-off by her father, whose idealism, Mrs. Trollope reports in the novel, left its mark on his daughter. In White's novel, we meet her when she is still a young woman, after she has made her first trip to America, where she is inspired by its vision of equality and respectful of its early experiments in democracy. Like the historical Wright, White's character is an early feminist, an outspoken abolitionist, atheist, and—later in life—champion of workers' rights. Equally notable, in the course of her many trips to the United States, Wright became the first woman to speak publicly about such issues and write about them as co-editor of the *New Harmony Gazette*, a newspaper published at the utopian community of New Harmony, Indiana, in the 1830s.

After her first trip to America, Wright published her *Views of Society and Manners in America* (1821), a book redolent of praise for the new land and its people. And shortly thereafter she set up one of America's earliest utopian communities, the Nashoba Commune, outside present-day Memphis,

Tennessee. A community dedicated to reforming social ideas about women as well as marriage and the family (both of which Wright opposed), Nashoba was denigrated by outsiders for what they mistakenly saw as its advocacy of free love, which helped contribute to its demise within a few years. At Nashoba, Wright also put into practice a plan for eliminating slavery, which she rightly saw as a blot on America's egalitarian experiment. It was Wright's idea that slaves be allowed to work to buy their freedom from slave owners who, if they did not have a moral right to own human beings, might best be placated, she thought, by a respect for their economic investment in their slaves.

In real life and in White's novel, Frances Trollope had more modest prospects than Wright. Consigned initially to a provincial domestic life outside London at Harrow, England, she had six children and a husband who was apparently incapable of supporting his family. Much of the burden of maintaining the home and educating the children fell to her, and in White's telling of her tale, once she becomes friends with the firebrand Fanny Wright, she follows the reformer to Nashoba in an effort to create some opportunity for herself and her children. But when she discovers that Nashoba is not quite the utopia Wright has represented it as being, she resettles for several years in Cincinnati, where she ventures upon several failed but highly original schemes to support her family. Trollope, unlike Wright, was disillusioned by America, and eventually returned to England where she wrote the highly critical polemic, *Domestic Manners of the Americans* (1832). The book made her famous and helped launch her into a successful new career as a bestselling novelist. If in the end her success seemed somewhat surer than Frances Wright's, the feminist scholar Elaine Showalter pointedly notes that "the two Fannys represented opposite extremes of 19th-century womanhood": "feminist and matriarch, radical and conservative, pro-American and anti-American, reformer and bestseller."[8] In many ways, White sets up Trollope as a counter to Wright's utopian idealism to bring into focus a crucial, and as we will see, unresolved tension in the novel: the question of whether genuine social change comes about through radical thought or individual action.

Fanny Wright's idealism is a major theme of the novel, which nevertheless sees such idealism as difficult to sustain and even perhaps unresponsive to people's lived social experience. Writing about his own novel, White himself says that "like so many radicals of the 1960s, Frances Wright had abandoned her principles and ended up deeply unhappy."[9] We see some of the paradoxes of her life most clearly in her marriage. Despite her distrust of the institution, she weds a man to keep her daughter from being illegitimate. But her husband, because of laws that do not permit married women to retain control of their own money, ruins her financially. And Mrs. Trollope—rather than maintain the biographer's attitude of detached observation—becomes increasingly competitive in her relationship to Wright and extremely critical. The pressing problem of such idealism as Wright's may very well be, as Trollope announces early in the work, that "an Idea is always more tenacious than a Reality,"[10] by which she seems to mean that, once people invest in an idea about something, it is difficult to reconcile that idea with cold, hard facts. Throughout the novel we see many of Fanny Wright's and others' most idealistic schemes come to naught because they have seemingly failed to account for the experiences and expectations of the people they are intended to benefit.

The Nashoba Commune, for instance, fails because it depends upon a scheme to have slaves buy their freedom and then be shipped back to Africa or Haiti. Wright is convinced by Thomas Jefferson (ironically, given the historical Jefferson's likely relationship with his slave Sally Hemmings) that there will never be any rapprochement between black and white Americans in the New World. But Fanny Trollope reports after her visit to Nashoba that "Fanny's great idea of freeing [the slaves] only to send them all back to Africa terrified them. . . . They spoke no African languages and their white masters had mixed them systematically for generations so that they would not be able to preserve either their African religion nor their native customs. Obviously they were in no hurry to buy their freedom if that meant exile" (183). Later, when Wright does transport the former slaves from Nashoba to the newly independent republic of Haiti, the promise of their success is mixed at best. What Wright, in her idealism, seems to ignore is that the "African" slaves have become, like many immigrants to the United States, fully American.

Rather than trumpeting radical notions, Mrs. Trollope emerges as a woman whose sense of the world changes in response to her individual experience of people. Revealing—indeed reveling in—her bias as a biographer, she contrasts what she calls Fanny's "Fanaticism" to her own "Sweet Moderation" (279). So, whereas Fanny Wright champions abolition but seems unable to feel personal sympathy for the slaves at Nashoba, Trollope observes in the African Americans she meets the genuine human feelings and aspiration the system of slavery has attempted unsuccessfully to eradicate. It is Trollope who notices the affections of a "Negro couple" at Nashoba when the man tenderly nurses a wound his partner has received, which leads her to observe that "it occurred to me that Negroes were kinder amongst themselves than we whites were with one another" (186). Significantly Trollope's empathy leads to identification, as she imagines herself in the emotional space of an enslaved black woman, "I almost envied the poor woman, so loving was her partner" (186). The moment dramatizes a kind of human sympathy Fanny Wright is never able to achieve or understand, and it has a profound impact on Trollope who, over the course of her life in Cincinnati, becomes lovers with Cudjo, a former slave.

Nevertheless it is not clear that Trollope's practical individualism is more effective in creating social change than Wright's idealism, for Trollope recognizes, rightly, that she cannot share the news of her love for Cudjo with anyone. Her bitter recognition of the fact even becomes an occasion for her to chastise the idealism of Wright, when she says that she can't even tell "that flaming radical Frances Wright . . . for even if she might have embraced a slave she would have buried the act of human congress under obliterating abstractions and high-minded rhetoric" (286). Wright, she says, would be unable to understand the simple, emotional connection between two human beings without making it an occasion for theorizing about freedom. But Trollope's own individual actions are in many ways as isolating as Wright's radical thought: "I couldn't share my happy news with anyone. . . . No, I was alone with my America" (286). Individual acts of freedom do not create the space in which genuine social change comes about. Trollope's actions are too challenging to be spoken, except in secret.

Throughout his writing, White seems aware that social change comes about only when new social scripts are invented to enable it. People have to learn to think differently before they will be enabled to act differently. Despite its democratic posturing, however, America refuses to sanction a proper social place for the kind of unconventional, individually fulfilling love Trollope finds with Cudjo: "Of course it was obvious, but I'd never meditated on the truth before that a real friendship between a Negro man and a white woman could occur only in the most stifling privacy, one that was equivalent to an admission of something shameful. There were no social forms or forums to house our feelings" (271).

Mrs. Trollope senses that her individual action cannot lead to social change because it remains private, and it cannot lead to personal growth because it is instituted as shame. In the end, Cudjo and Mrs. Trollope leave each other and both leave America. Their relationship is as fractured as the one Frances Wright experiences with the slaves she delivered to Haiti. Separated by international borders, they all (except Fanny Wright, who dies soon thereafter) seek private happiness outside America.

What becomes increasingly clear in *Fanny* is that the limitations of both Frances Wright's and Frances Trollope's approaches to progressive social understanding are shaped by contradictions inherent in American life. The novel characterizes the United States as a place where the ideal of equality is championed in distinction to a sadder reality. Nowhere is this contradiction clearer than in the manifest hypocrisies of slavery and American racism, which are persistent themes. There is hardly a character in the novel—with the exception of Trollope—able to accept without question the humanity of the novel's black characters. Even Fanny Wright, who initially urges the dissolution of the races through intermarriage, succumbs as we saw to Thomas Jefferson's belief that American slaves need to be sent "somewhere—back to Africa or to California or Haiti or Texas. Somewhere. The races were not meant to live together" (98). That White does not expect us to take this kind of thinking at face value is evident because of his invention of the love affair between Trollope and Cudjo. It is a clear instance in which the author shapes a modern ideal in conscious distinction to historical reality. Mrs. Trollope's and Cudjo's affair represents the history that might or ought to have been rather than the history that was allowed to be in America.

Nor is White's view of the social stratification within America's newly emergent democracy limited to race. Class and status become powerful markers of hierarchy and difference. The indefatigable Mrs. Trollope, brilliant and responsive but poor and poorly dressed, frequently notes her exclusion from the newer forms of classed society emerging in the States. The novel exposes as well the hypocrisies of that great hero of the American Revolution, the French marquis, General Lafayette. Notwithstanding his commitment to American democracy, Trollope characterizes him as a man who remains obsessed with European notions of aristocracy—a conclusion with which Wright comes to concur. The children of George Washington conspire with the children of Lafayette to shut Fanny Wright out of their lives, clinging as they do to aristocratic notions of class superiority. But even Fanny Wright is not immune. In a devastating indictment toward the end of the novel, Trollope says that Fanny, unlike most people in America, was "genuinely color-blind." Still, "she was totally unalive to the feelings and actions of her ex-slaves. She didn't see them, not because they were black but because they were humble" (322). The novel almost seems to suggest that America's problem with race is related to its inability to eliminate social hierarchy and that, as such, it is intractable.

Perhaps the picture of America that emerges in *Fanny* can be summed up by words of the real Mrs. Trollope repeated by White's character when she calls Cincinnati, White's childhood home, "this triste little town," where there was no "culture [or] pleasure of any sort" (232). Learning in America is something "Americans prefer to utilize . . . rather than possess" (237). Mrs. Trollope seems to mean that Americans are distrustful of theoretical knowledge that might lead to meaningful thought and change. These are, of

course, the character's observations and not necessarily White's, and ironically Mrs. Trollope is guilty of a similar distrust, as her characterization of
Fanny Wright shows. But when her ideas are viewed against a background
of stifling American provinciality and social hypocrisy, the brilliant idealism
of all the social reformers in *Fanny*—Wright, Robert Owen, and Frances
Trollope—seems all the more necessary and noble, even if, as White makes
clear, its chances for success are limited. For America as it is portrayed in
the novel is a land where personalities prosper so that idealism itself can be
rooted out.

Despite her objections to Fanny Wright, even Trollope seems genuinely
angry at the way America forgets her almost immediately after her death:
"Considering she was the first woman in America to speak publicly against
slavery, the first woman ever to address a mixed audience, a notorious atheist, the first leader of the first labor party, the most radical journalist in the
land, the oblivion that swallowed her whole is a stunning (I could say *deliberate*) act of effacement. She was too challenging, too uncomfortable to be
remembered. In any event Americans denigrate ideas by attaching them to
colorful personalities, whom they decide should be replaced by new, even
more bizarre eccentrics" (336–37).

Given that White himself has championed causes of sexual liberation
that in their own time and place may have seemed as extreme as Wright's
ideas, we might hear Mrs. Trollope's words as a defense of radical idealism
and freedom in the face of America's betrayal of its originary ideals. Indeed,
that the novel resurrects for its reader's pleasure two otherwise forgotten
women, whose contributions to America's understanding of itself have been
largely neglected and forgotten, suggests that White creates it, in part, to
resist actively and brilliantly that tendency in American life, as Mrs. Trollope
identifies it, to ignore, erase, and neglect what makes it uncomfortable.

We might best understand *Fanny*, then, as an attempt to resist such erasure by recalling people and ideas—even if they are fictionalized—who were
involved in creating what Mrs. Trollope called, in reference to her love
for Cudjo, the "social forms" and public "forums" necessary to "house"
unconventional ideas (271). Both Fannies have a great deal in common with
the protagonists of White's earlier fictions who struggle to give shape and
embodiment to a place for their own unconventional desires—sexual and
otherwise—within the conventional outlines of American provincial life.

Still, we will not fully understand *Fanny* without taking some account of
its form and structure, which provide something of a melancholic or even
tragic gloss to the whole. No matter that Frances Trollope is a wholly engag-
ing speaker, she proves herself to be a largely unreliable narrator of the life

of Frances Wright. By the end of the novel Trollope confesses to key gaps in her understanding of Wright. It is "an entertaining reversal in the action" that reminds us "that there is more than one way to tell a story."[11] The point is made vividly in a séance Trollope orchestrates in the work's closing pages as part of her research for a new novel. Fanny Wright appears unexpectedly to denounce her as a liar and "profiteer" (363). Whereas Trollope has suggested throughout that Wright was having sex with the many powerful men who aided her progressive schemes, the ghostly Wright accuses her of sullying all her accomplishments through this and similar insinuations. In fact, in looking back over the pages of Trollope's "biography," we might discern the author's apparent jealousy and growing animosity for Wright, which does not provide the ideal stance for a biographer. Ultimately we cannot be sure how much she tells us about Wright is or is not true. In fact, Trollope's "biography" of Fanny turns out to be better as a confessional autobiography, one that reveals its subject, Trollope, in all her rich successes and vain imaginings.

In creating this formal structure that folds in upon itself—that is, that allows Trollope to aggrandize herself by criticizing her subject—White cleverly reveals the subtle problems of Fanny Wright's radical idealism. He also, however, demonstrates how conventional individualists such as Trollope might contribute to the erasure of a radical past they are entirely dependent on. Understood rightly, there would be no Mrs. Trollope without Frances Wright, for it is Wright's utopian schemes that bring Trollope to America and Wright's concern with the problem of race that leads Trollope to rethink her racist ideas and find love with Cudjo. Too little in Trollope's "biography" acknowledges these debts. One might wonder if Trollope isn't like one of those very Americans she fails to admire, a self-promoting individualist overly dependent on practical knowledge to gain advancement.

It is around questions of sexuality especially that Trollope seems most fallible as a narrator. There is a running joke concerning the French painter Auguste Hervieu and Trollope's son Henry. Hervieu is a friend of the Trollopes who goes to America with Mrs. Trollope and saves her and her family financially on several occasions. He is clearly having an affair with Henry—a fact that Wright discerns immediately. Trollope, however, vainly imagines that Hervieu is devoted, secretly, to her. Surely this failure to see sex clearly even in her own family is related to her inability to parse Frances Wright's sexual relations. It signals something else as well. Both in her failure to understand her son's sexual difference and her inability to fully parse the complexities of Wright's sexual idealism, Trollope seems inevitably to judge sex within the norms of conventional romance and family life. So, despite her own personal courage within that tradition, she persistently belittles and erases radical possibilities in others' thought and actions. In this sense, *Fanny,* a historical novel about the nineteenth century, reflects tensions that continue to exist in alternative sexual and other communities in America in the twenty-first century. Radical theorists and pioneering individualists continue to struggle over who best promotes social change. White's novel seems to suggest one needs both, people who articulate new social forms and people with the courage to begin living them. In this way, *Fanny* provides an explicit political gloss to the processes of social change recorded in many of White's novels.

Hotel de Dream

As with *Fanny,* critics of *Hotel de Dream* focused on the act of literary ventriloquism White performed in this novel within a novel. The framing story concerns the last days of the great American naturalist-realist writer Stephen Crane, who died of tuberculosis in 1900 at age twenty-eight. Within this frame, the fictional Crane tells of a novel he had written several years earlier about a boy-prostitute in New York City, an ostensible companion piece to the real Crane's famous story of a girl's fall into prostitution in *Maggie: A Girl of the Streets* (1893). After a chance encounter with the teenaged Elliott, who, like Maggie, supports himself as a prostitute, Crane writes a novel that he is advised to burn by the eminent American author Hamlin Garland. Garland considers it too shocking, and fears it will ruin Crane's emerging reputation as one of America's great writers. In his last days, however, with nothing left to lose, Crane returns to the story of Elliott to re-create it, and White structures this emerging story in between his tale of Crane's slow death. Titled "The Painted Boy," this novella is White's imitation of Stephen Crane, a man who, like White himself, was a notable literary stylist.

White does not entirely fabricate this story about Crane's manuscript. As he makes clear in a "Postface" to the novel, there has been found among the papers of Crane's first biographer, Thomas Beer, a "single piece of paper" that records the words of Crane's friend, the New York critic James Gibbon Huneker.[12] Huneker says he was with Crane in the spring of 1894 when they ran into a boy prostitute or "painted" boy (224). Crane was initially disturbed and sickened by the boy, but fed him and helped him get treatment for his syphilis. Later, Huneker claims, Crane "began a novel" about such a boy, the beginning scene of which was "probably the best passage of prose that Crane ever wrote" (224). But when he showed the work to Garland, the critic was "horrified and begged him to stop. I don't know," Huneker writes, "that he ever finished the book" (224). As White makes clear, Crane's early biographer, Thomas Beer, was not above forging documents about Crane or ones supposedly written by him, and because there is no external evidence for this lost book by Stephen Crane, its former or present existence cannot be supposed true. So, *Hotel de Dream*, White writes, "is my fantasia on real themes provided by history" (223). While it records many of the key facts about the last days of Stephen Crane, its central story about his encounter with a boy prostitute, his writing a novel about that boy, and the substance of the novella itself are literary inventions.

While many, not all, of the initial reviewers of *Fanny* agreed that White had managed to create a credible imitation of Frances Trollope's literary voice, which they took to be one of *Fanny*'s charms, they have been less charitable to *Hotel de Dream*—or, more strictly speaking, to "The Painted Boy." Some find it to be a reasonable approximation of Crane's style. The novelist Sophie Gee reviewing for the *New York Times* applauds White for his "remarkable feats of stylistic impersonation" and for "the descriptions of New York's thieves, vagrants and whores [that] have [a] stomach-turning realism."[13] Others doubt that White, himself a master of nuance, has captured the precise subtleties of Crane, "who was a precursor to Hemingway, writing in visual images and respecting masculine inarticulacy."[14] Historian Eric Homberger suggests that "Crane observed passion from an ironic height, and had nothing to say of the breasts or any other body-part of his heroine [Maggie]." "White," however, "is enamoured of the erotics of skin and penis, and dwells upon sexual obsession. It is hard to imagine two writers more unlike."[15]

Notwithstanding these real or imagined failures, the point of White's novel seems not to be to create an exact literary impersonation so much as to write back into American history and literature the sex, homosexual desire, and homosexual passion that have been largely erased from both. Because of his interest in powerless, displaced people and the rumor of his own lost manuscript, Crane provides a convenient jumping-off point for White's historical project. In this regard, *Hotel de Dream* rejects the fear of Henry James (a great American novelist and friend of Crane who makes a significant appearance in the novel) that historical fiction cannot accurately represent "the old CONSCIOUSNESS, the soul, the sense" of the past.[16] On the contrary, as Christopher Benfey notes, "projecting ourselves into the past isn't a peril of the enterprise of historical fiction, as James thought; it *is* the enterprise."[17] *Hotel de Dream* is a "fantasia," a fantasy in which, White writes in the "Postface," he tries to imagine his own answers to a few deceptively simple

questions: "How would a heterosexual man who had wide human sympa-
thies, an affection for prostitutes, a keen, compassionate curiosity about the
poor and downtrodden, a terminal disease—how would such a man have
responded to male homosexuality if he was confronted with it? How would
he have thought about it in an era when homosexuals themselves were grop-
ing for explanations of their proclivities?" (225–26).

In this sense, White's novel puts homosexuality back into American literature and history much as the author's earlier autobiographical novels placed
gay characters on the scene of American consciousness. Perhaps it points to
some more challenging questions as well: what does it mean that Crane could
write about Maggie, a girl of the streets, without speaking about her body?
And why have we accepted that version of history as "realism," both in its
literary and literal senses? As we have seen, the body and the ways it shapes
experience and desire are central themes of White's fiction, so it should come
as no surprise that he highlights the body in *Hotel de Dream*, both in the
framing story and in his novel-within-a-novel.

"The Painted Boy" points toward some of White's most important
themes: the revelation of gay lives in America and the ways they are mis-
shaped by American cultural ignorance, homophobia, and hypocrisy; the
importance of sex and desire in the lives of individuals; and the pleasures and
perils of the body. It is about a young man, Elliott, who is a prostitute on
the streets of New York in the 1890s. Elliott has fled an abusive family situation in upstate New York and lands in the city, where he meets Silas Aspen,
a news distributor who sets him up as a newspaper deliver boy. Silas runs a
service on the side in which Elliott hand delivers a paper to particular men
who "wanted a paper delivered with benefits, that is 'a kiss and a cuddle,'"
for which he is paid extra (65).

Notably White does not portray Elliott or his circumstances as the worst
he could suffer—that, apparently, was his home life to which Elliott has no
desire to return—and there is a great deal of dignity in the boy who makes
his own way in a strange and demanding world. Morris Dickstein justly
sees White's novel-within-a-novel as a Horatio Alger story. "It has all the
Alger ingredients: An abused farm boy from upstate arrives in New York
City, becomes a newsboy and urban waif, but falls under the protection of
a respectable middle-aged man who becomes his mentor."[18] Along the way
(both here and in the framing story), White resurrects a history of homosexuality in early New York, its language and its codes, and so sheds light on a
"queer community that necessarily lived in the shadows and that has gone
largely unacknowledged until recently."[19] He also provides evidence of odd

but decent nurturing figures among the unconventional sexual inhabitants of New York, most notably Jennie June, an intersexed character who befriends and helps guide Elliott through his new life.

The gist of the story, however, concerns Elliott's relationship with Theodore, a respectable married man who falls in love with the boy and sets him up in an apartment where they can be together. Theodore is willing to risk everything for Elliott. He is a man who wants exactly what conventional America will not give him: the love of his wife and children in addition to Elliott. Indeed, considering the sexless state of his marriage, what Theodore wants is in part the satisfaction of a physical intimacy that is curtailed on every level of his middle-class American life. White explores here, as he does elsewhere, intergenerational desire, seeing it in terms of an economic relationship that may have been more common than we like to think in the 1890s—the exchange of sexual intimacy for financial gain and domestic security. But while today such relationships are perhaps only respectably imagined in fantasy (as in *Caracole*) or at a historical remove (as here), White presses the limits of received wisdom to boldly suggest that this sexual economy does not lie outside the bounds of legitimate love and desire. Indeed, Elliott and Theodore's relationship as it is portrayed in the novel constitutes an exchange that reflects the value of the youth's body as well as the legitimacy of the older man's feelings, without reducing either to simple materiality.

"The Painted Boy," then, is clearly not a novel about conventional forms of gay desire; it is, rather, a story about the social proscriptions on homosexual desire in America. Given the available social scripts for understanding homosexuality in Crane's time, it necessarily ends tragically, with Theodore exposed and ruined and Elliott horribly disfigured, burned in a fire. Crane doesn't finish the novel, but he leaves instructions with his partner Cora to ask Henry James to do so. Hoping to extract some dignity for his lovers, the sympathetic Crane suggests that James should conclude with Theodore and Elliott "alone in the sitting room with [a] statue" of Elliott's youthful body that Theodore had had sculpted before the boy's disfigurement (217). But James, fearing, as Garland did before him, that it will be a blot on Crane's literary reputation, burns this new manuscript.

To appreciate the significance of this rather melodramatic tale, we need to see it in relation to the framing narrative. In some ways, the story of Crane's last days reverses the situation of "The Painted Boy," in which White imagines a heterosexual author writing about a homosexual relationship. Here we find Edmund White, a gay man, meditating on the love between Stephen Crane and Cora, itself a rather unconventional relationship because Cora is a former prostitute and proprietress of a bordello in Jacksonville, Florida, the Hotel de Dream. Although Cora lives with Crane as his wife, they are not formally married. White takes the hotel's name as his title perhaps because it valorizes the dreams of both sets of unconventional lovers but also because it points ironically to the ways they both exist within a private dream-state outside the narrow norms of American society. Not only is White concerned with legitimizing homosexual and heterosexual relationships that others would simply dismiss, but he seems interested in exploring the ways they are and are not alike.

The framing narrative itself is almost literally a meditation—for there is very little action in it. It begins with Crane sick and bedridden at his home in Sussex, England, where he is tended by Cora, and it ends with Crane's death in Germany, where Cora has taken him for treatment. Aside from a few scenes detailing the difficulties of traveling and a witty fictionalization of a visit the real Crane might have received from Henry James, the primary narrative of *Hotel de Dream* consists of Crane's intimate dealings with Cora and his memories of their past lives. Exploring once again the theme of memory, White shows Crane attempting to understand his life by recollecting his past. It is within this recollection that we discover the genesis of "The Painted Boy," so that we might wonder what Crane's great desire to complete the novel before he dies reveals about his present situation.

One answer, the simplest one perhaps, is that his desire to write his novel allows Crane to maintain a hold on life and a degree of self-assertion even as his body fails. The question of writing—what it creates and secures in terms of one's place in the world—and the question of the body—what it means for one's place—are always important ones in White's work. And as in White's other works, the two questions overlap in *Hotel de Dream*. Not only does the novel reflect the effects of a young man's decline from a gradually debilitating disease—a situation White has dealt with in those fictions based on his lover Hubert Sorin's death from AIDS—but it imagines the death of an author. Consequently the novel takes up questions about the relationship of death and the practice of writing that have also concerned White, especially in *Chaos* but also in *The Farewell Symphony*, where the production of a novel serves to memorialize the dead.

In this particular case, Crane's interest in Elliott seems to stem in part from a desire to tell the truth in the face of what he sees as the "banal decency" of renditions of conventional boyhood in other writers such as Hamlin Garland (10). His sympathy for Elliott proceeds from his awareness that he "had to carry him through a sea of disapproval" (14), so that his defense of the boy projects his own sense of power both as a man whose body is failing and as

a writer committed to a version of the truth. Cora understands Crane's obsessive focus on producing "The Painted Boy" as being a highly veiled attempt
to revisit "the vital kid he'd once been" (92). It is an effort to recapture that
masculine power being eroded by his new dependence on his wife by asking
her to "witness" his interest in "an all-male world" (93).

In all these senses, White meditates in *Hotel de Dream* on a traditional
understanding that writing confers immortality, albeit in this case with his
own take on the idea. Writing materially embodies the power that is otherwise threatened by the death of the writer. *Hotel de Dream* is, after all, a
novel that literally produces another novel within its frame, that is, it makes
the story of Elliott literal in the creation of "The Painted Boy." Obviously
as well, this assertion of the power of writing is related to the reproduction
of homosexuality within the framework of American history and literature.
Elliott, whom White painstakingly creates in great detail as an exemplar of
a type of homosexual life in the 1890s in New York City, would be lost to
history without Crane's novel because, as we have seen, his death is prefig-
ured already in his syphilis and he has no power to tell his own story. That
the statue of his boyish body remains is small consolation, but the symbol
prefigures Crane's (and White's) writing him into historical existence. There
is perhaps no clearer moment in White's fiction of the connection between
writing and the legitimation of sexuality, homosexuality, and the body that
has been an abiding concern of his work. White enlists Crane, the great
genius and sympathetic American chronicler of American street life, in his
own project that, in essence, continues in Crane's vein.

White consolidates this idea in his witty and (in many ways unfair) send-
up of another of his own great predecessors, the American novelist Henry
James. James himself has long been understood to have displaced his awareness of sex and his own sexual desires into a highly nuanced analysis of the
social workings of society. James's prose style is highly evasive and rarely
concrete, and it becomes in the novel—especially in the down-to-earth Cora's
commentary on it—an evasion of the body and its pleasures and meanings.
Cora recognizes that James is "not the sort of individual" who frequented
the bordello, the Hotel de Dream, that she ran before she started living with
Crane (38). James, she believes, is attracted to her husband, but he "never
gave into his impulses—he wouldn't hug or kiss the poor, thin sweating Stevie" (38).

Not surprisingly, then, White leaves it to James at the end of the novel
to once again consign the manuscript of "The Painted Boy" to the fire, for
he comes to stand as a symbol of a literary and cultural establishment (that
includes, of course, Hamlin Garland) intent on removing not just the body

but homosexuality from consideration. James is, of course, a great writer in his own right, but the displacement of sex in his writing serves White as an appropriate literary sign of the ways a homophobic society erases homosexuality and sex from literature, thus necessitating White's own re-creation of that record. Authoring "The Painted Boy" is an assertion of power by two authors whose bodies are failing them: the dying Crane and the aging White.

Perhaps, however, the emotional heart of *Hotel de Dream* is to be found in its framing story. In his depiction of the relationship between Cora and the dying Crane, White reveals a deep understanding of and sympathy for a love many would dismiss as unconventional. On an obvious level, Crane's novel raises issues about the power dynamics of romantic and sexual attachments, what Cora calls "the hydraulics of desire" in words that echo *Nocturnes for the King of Naples* (41).[20] We have already seen her interpret Crane's book about an all-male world as a way for him to contest her power over his sick and dying body. We might note as well the ways the novel highlights her insecurities as the partner of Crane, whom she knows to have proposed to another woman, Lily, before settling permanently with her. Cora fears that her situation is somewhat like Theodore's wife, Christine. She worries that Crane feels "love and respect" for her but not the kind of passion that he felt for Lily or that Theodore feels for Elliott (198). If we recall the pathos Crane, a heterosexual man, felt for Theodore and Elliott in "The Painted Boy," we might imagine that here White reveals, perhaps from his perspective as a gay man, that heterosexual relationships can also be made both more insecure and perhaps more profoundly felt by the realization that erotic desire always potentially plays across multiple bodies.

In other words, love is not (or not only) figured in conventionally monogamous forms. Cora shares Stephen with his book, with Henry James, and possibly with Lily. There is a possible gender inequity in the novel's representation of Cora, for we are not treated to as extensive an analysis of those loves with whom Stephen shares his wife—although her former life as a prostitute suggests that Stephen has shared his wife's affections. But the point is that for White, erotic relationships are, characteristically, subtle and complicated compounds of intimacy and distance, the push and pull of functioning machinery, to pick up on Cora's metaphor.

Nor does White back away from a central awareness in all his novels that love—gay and straight—is physical, that it unfolds across bodies. Theodore's desire for Elliott is not portrayed as shallow but profoundly intimate. Elliott's words suggest, too, that it is not exploitative but nurturing: "No one is as good and kind as you," Elliott tells Theodore. "Why would I leave you?" (102). Indeed, the lovers' easy-going physicality reflects that of Cora and

Crane. On several occasions, White imagines Crane being attracted to Cora because he feels "free" with her, but also "naked and vulnerable" (127, 128). She is "wonderfully companionable, frank as a boy and relaxed as a sister" (128). It is perhaps a singularly male fantasy of sexual camaraderie, but White suggests that it is bodily familiarity rather than idealized emotion that connects the two. Cora's own freedom about the body enables her to make one of the most profound and moving statements in the novel, when Stephen, utterly wracked, says he is ashamed for having pissed himself in bed. "Why on earth?" she asks. "It's just the poor body, Stevie, that's failing" (196). On the surface, her words seem to contradict White's faith in the body, especially when she contrasts it to Crane's "immortal spirit" (196). But the body for White is not a metaphysical marker—and certainly not a sign for shame. Here and elsewhere in his work, it is a conduit of significant love and human interaction that is merely—and always—susceptible to physical failure. This may be one of White's most important—and enduring—themes.

Indeed, once Stephen dies, Cora wants nothing more to do with the wasted body that is left to her. It is a "burnt-out hive" (218). She thinks of it as a "reproach," reminding her that "she'd been given a precious possession . . . and she had let it drop from her hands" (218). One doesn't, of course, walk away from death without remorse and guilt. Still, there is little in the ending of the novel that argues for love as a type of transcendent force beyond the physical. So however we interpret the particular weight of the body against more traditional idealizations of love, *Hotel de Dream* suggests that physical connection through the body is neither a poor substitute for nor a step on the path to some less worldly connection. The novel celebrates what it is in itself. If "The Painted Boy" puts homosexuality back into an American literature and history that had effaced it, *Hotel de Dream* belongs to that tradition of modern (and modernist) novels that returns sex and the body as well.

CHAPTER SIX

Late Works

Chaos and *Jack Holmes and His Friend*

Edmund White's latest fiction (as of the writing of this chapter) retreats from the distant historical concerns of *Fanny* and *Hotel de Dream,* but nevertheless reflects some of the apparent dissatisfactions with autobiography that prompted the author's turn to history in the first place. If, as White says, his historical fiction gave him a way to write novels that were not about himself, his most recent work also suggests that autobiographical modes may no longer suffice to express his vision. One critic has written that White's autobiographical short-fiction collection, *Chaos: A Novella and Stories* (2007), feels flat and lacking in energy, as if White has exhausted the form.[1] But looked at more carefully—and seen in the hindsight of *Jack Holmes and His Friend*—White seems to be exploring autobiographical form itself, comprehending what cannot be said in the voices of aging narrators whose bodies are deteriorating and whose memories are becoming exhausted. *Chaos* calls into question the utility of writing and memory for finding meaning in one's experience—the very presuppositions upon which much of White's earlier autobiographical work had been based. As the title novella suggests, the threat of emotional and intellectual chaos looms large for White's characters.

Jack Holmes and His Friend (2012) is more complicated, and represents some resolution to the formal tensions apparent in *Chaos*. It is a historical novel about the 1960s and 1970s,[2] and like any good historical novel, it excavates and uncovers a time past with the goal of illuminating the present. But the past White returns to is recognizably his own, and while the characters he develops are obviously not avatars of White himself, they often have some of the attributes of those earlier autobiographical characters who are. If, as White writes in the acknowledgments, *Jack Holmes* represents "a new way of writing a novel,"[3] that way is one in which the author thinks more abstractly about the meanings to be derived from the historical circumstances in which he lived without personalizing them. The difference explains, perhaps, why this novel ends as no other novel by White does, with even its gay characters partnered and content. The ending does not reflect White's own more complex understanding of emotional and sexual relations (at least as we've come to understand them in his earlier work) so much as his sense of how particular characters might have conducted their lives at a specific time in history. As a historical fiction, *Jack Holmes and His Friend* reflects a dominant sentiment of the time about which White writes, when the advent of AIDS in the United States led many to argue for an end to the sexual free-for-all of the 1970s and a return to traditional partner arrangements or, at the least, serial monogamy.

Chaos

Chaos includes the novella from which the book takes its title and three stories, "Record Time," "Give It Up For Billy," and "Good Sport." In a later, paperback edition published in London in 2010, White included two previously unpublished stories, "A Modern Odyssey," and "The Creative Writing Murders." Initially, *Chaos* seems incoherent as a collection, an impression exacerbated by the additional stories in the British edition. But many of these short fictions are concerned with memory and its decay along with the aging bodies of their characters. In these stories, written as White approached his seventies, aging renders one's experience of and grasp on the significance of one's life tenuous indeed.

The collection opens with the title novella, in which a sixty-six-year-old author, Jack, describes the chaos his life seems to be descending into as he ages and copes with the imminent death in Paris of his best friend, Marie-Hélène, from whom he is separated by the Atlantic Ocean. Jack has money problems due to a declining interest in the kinds of literary work he produces: in the course of the novella, his editor rejects his latest novel and a friend in the business pointedly tells him as far as publishing is concerned, "Read my lips: No. More. Gays. No. More. Novels."[4] This is devastating news to an author who, like White himself, has built his career on creating a literature that documented the rise of gay life in America. His only consolation seems to be found in the genuinely affectionate sexual relationships he establishes with two younger men, Seth and Giuseppe, a consolation nevertheless mitigated by the fact that both relationships involve Jack's paying for their sexual favors, which highlights not only the decline of his physical desirability but his ability to pay.

White remains typically iconoclastic in his explicit representation of intergenerational sex, and his insistence that the exchange of cash is only to be expected if one is to maintain a vigorous sex life at an advanced age. And, as usual, he doesn't succumb to conventional verities suggesting that the exchange of money precludes genuine affection. The pleasure one obtains from reading the story derives perhaps from watching Jack juggle these various chaotic issues that never cohere into anything like a comprehensive statement about the meaning of life, even though at the end Seth writes an email message to Jack that calls him out, both with affection and cruelty, for a certain self-serving, self-pitying attitude that obscures the ways he has remained more successful and vital than he is willing to concede. Reprinting Seth's message as a type of coda, Jack is able to tell the story of his own decline and at the same time revel in his remaining powers, even in old age.

"Give it Up for Billy" and "A Good Sport" both concern older characters whose lives are revealed in similarly ironic ways. In the first case, Harold, a sixty-three-year-old history professor at Princeton returns to his favorite winter retreat, Key West, where he has a brief affair with Billy, a go-go boy at a local bar. Although Harold is envied by others for his good luck in finding Billy, the story turns on the question of how and in what ways the relationship is exploitative. Because Billy is from Zimbabwe during the Mugabe era, Harold wrongly assumes he has come to America to enjoy freedom as a gay man. He regards paying Billy for sex as contributing to his possibilities for freedom.

But when he learns that Billy is married, it occurs to him that perhaps Billy had never been gay at all and had prostituted himself out of genuine need to raise money to relocate his family in Africa—although the realization leads only to rationalization: "A small, peevish voice somewhere inside of him said, 'See? He was just using you and everyone else.' But then Harold smiled, pleased at the simplifying form things had taken" (140). The story raises questions about who uses whom, and what the stakes of such use are. While it seems not to take up the usual moral condemnations of using money to obtain sex, the story does question Harold's ethical awareness and indeed that of all people whose sexual lives turn on a privileged freedom they rather naively assume to be available to all, even those in dire social circumstances. In this, it brilliantly complicates celebrations of sexual freedom to be found elsewhere in White's work.

"A Good Sport" returns to one of White's great themes, friendship, as it describes the long-term relationship between the nameless narrator, a

seventy-one-year-old Latinist retired from the University of Chicago, and the
woman he is now living with, Helena, in Naxos on Crete. As the narrator
describes his life and friendship with Helena, he returns to a story that took
place twenty years earlier when he and Helena rented a house on an island
near Istanbul. The son of the owner of the house, Davud, becomes something
of their constant companion, and while Helena believes he is courting her, he
is, in fact, sneaking with great regularity to the narrator's bedroom throughout the summer of their habitation in Istanbul. The narrator tells this story
from his present life in Naxos, when his opium addiction prevents him from
knowing securely which details of the story he tells are accurate. At the end,
Helena throws his opium stash down the toilet, demanding that he "come
back to the present," and comically insisting that if he's "going to dwell on
the past it should at least be a *viable memory*" (184). The joke, of course,
is that no memory can be "viable" in the sense of being hard, factual, and
attuned to present realities.

Finally, "Record Time" is a beautiful nostalgia piece about the loneliness
of the narrator at age thirteen. But it is not simply "empty" loneliness or
self-conscious separation from the pack that the story describes. Rather it is
a "full, self-sufficient kind" in which the young narrator immerses himself
in a world of books, records, and imaginative play (101, 102). The narrator
mockingly refers to himself as a "self-invented Midwestern public-library
intellectual who ate books and records and art reproductions the way other
people ate meat and potatoes" (109). Still, "Record Time" suggests that the
boy's engagement with art and culture is the lonely substance of a youth
that will inevitably pass when at the end the narrator, returning home from
a screening of Greta Garbo's *Camille*, writes that "I opened my window and
toasted the wet spring night, which didn't feel like the beginning of anything
but the very last plucked note at the end of a long, soft, slow coda" (114).
The story is a mood piece in which memory renders the past fully formed to
the present.

In his earlier work, White seemed assured that memory provided not
only the building blocks of fiction but the key to understanding one's experience of the self. In these stories, neither memory nor fiction suffices. So, in
"Chaos" Jack worries that the audience for fiction is disappearing in the face
of technological entertainment. Although the optimistic Giuseppi tells him
that the internet revolution is fading and that "serious people, real people,
are returning to books, the real roots of their inner life" (84), Jack, shortly
thereafter, tells the story of a librarian at Kent State University who speaks
to him about a series of love letters in the library's possession that Jack had
written to a "famous New York theater director." The irony is that Jack

cannot remember the letters, his lover, or even that he had known the director at all (85). So much, the story suggests, for the "real roots" of his inner
life. Jack had "written so much and so fast and had always borrowed so hast-
ily, even crudely, from his own untransformed life, that he had no idea where
or whether he'd described any particular event or person" (85–86). Fiction,
as Jack writes early on, "was anxious work . . . designed to bring pleasure
or at least meaning to someone else in some place unknown to the author"
(4). Whether it brings pleasure and meaning to the author who cannot even
recall its relation to his own real experience seems up for grabs. Indeed, when
Seth reinterprets Jack's story in his own way at the end of "Chaos," we can
be pretty sure that neither memory nor fiction definitively settles one's understanding of self.

The point is similar to ones explored in "Give it Up for Billy" and "A
Good Sport." The protagonists of these stories, too, experience chaos at the
heart of their search for meaning—although Harold's moral obtuseness and
the opium addiction of the narrator of "A Good Sport" allow both characters to evade to some extent the fears resulting from their aging and declining
power. All these stories recording the pleasures of longstanding friendship,
intellectual conversation, and physical love promise to be, but are not, finally,
optimistic about the achievements of fiction, memory, and experience in confirming the validity of one's life. The exception may be "Record Time," but
that story is so perfectly realized as an expression of the narrator's past that
it begs the question of the meaning of memory and writing in understanding
the present. Except for those brief moments in which the narrator contextualizes how we are to think about different experiences of loneliness, the
past remains another country and fiction that pure artifact Jack describes in
"Chaos," something "written in the past tense and . . . lobbed like a paper
plane over a cliff toward an unknown destination" (4). This is not a comment on the quality of the story, which is first rate in its ability to move and
inform. It is, rather, a recognition of the melancholy that attends White's
understanding that fiction and memory may float free of the governing consciousness creating them.

The two stories added to the 2010 edition seem more loosely connected
to the others primarily because they do not reflect the concerns of aging
narrators. "A Modern Odyssey" does takes up the theme of the body and
its transformation in the story of an adolescent boy, Ulysses, who grows
up loving the gardener, Eumaius, at the estate on which he lives. When he
comes into his inheritance, he travels to Brazil to get a sex change, becomes
Odette, and then returns home to consummate his love for the gardener.
Although Odette assumes Eumaius does not recognize her, the story ends

with Eumaius's highly charged confession, "I liked you better as a boy."[5] Both a fantasy about the ability of love to transcend bodily transformation and a nod toward the tragedy of a person who imagines that love depends on a particular, gendered configuration of desire, "A Modern Odyssey" is about a Ulysses whose travels do not necessarily make him wiser. Its concerns, then, are not entirely inconsistent with those of the other stories in the book, which reflect tensions about an aging writer's relationship to his body and his own experience.

"The Creative Writing Murders" is a tale of sexual intrigue, murder, and academic maneuvering for limited power in the English Department at Wilford College, a provincial outpost on the terrain of American intellect. Its Hispanic narrator, Manuela, tells of a series of murders that take place that clear the way for her to assume a leadership role in the department. The story is punctuated by incoherent outbursts of seeming poetry, and Manuela rather schizophrenically confesses to hearing voices that "dictate" to her "what [she] should do next" (196). So, it never becomes entirely clear whether Manuela is telling in a neutral way the story of what actually happens or confessing, through writing, to involvement in a series of murders. Indeed, it is not clear that White's story is anything but one of Manuela's fictions, for she, too, is a writer. Wittily and complexly alluding to the ways writing can become a form of evasion rather than truth, "The Creative Writing Murders" parodies a demand that minority writers satisfy the intellectual establishment's appetite for tales about their so-called authentic experiences. Like "Chaos," it points toward a critical naïveté in readers who assume an over-easy connection between an author and his (or her) writings.

Jack Holmes and His Friend

The connection between author and writings is germane to understanding *Jack Holmes and His Friend*. White concedes that in this novel, which develops the realist tradition of his earlier autobiographical works, he nevertheless attempts to "enact [his] own dramas in other terms. . . . I tried . . . to give a character somewhat the trajectory of my life, going to the University of Michigan, coming to New York in '62, working for a big magazine and so on, but have him be an entirely different person. . . . It's kind of historical fiction in the sense that it's about the 60s and 70s; it's kind of autobiographical in that the character follows the same trajectory I did. But it's also imaginative in that the character is entirely different, and what he makes of his situation in life is quite different from what I made of mine."[6]

Jack Holmes and His Friend takes up a subject that has been present but not foregrounded in White's work from the beginning: the nature of

heterosexuality and its differences from homosexuality. It tells of an enduring albeit troubled bond of friendship between two men, one gay and one
straight, so that it becomes, as one reviewer puts it, a type of "Platonic
dialogue . . . about love and desire, gay and straight."[7] In this, it reflects the
growing complexity of White's analysis of desire and sexuality in American
life as a whole. The novel tells its story of the long-term friendship between
Jack Holmes and Will Wright in a more-or-less unified and chronological
way. Nevertheless White narrates the first and third sections of the novel in
third-person from the point of view of its gay character, Jack, and the second
part and epilogue in the first-person voice of Jack's straight friend, Will, who
Jack loves.

In a writer as concerned with creating voices of gay experience as White
has been throughout his career, the shift midway through this novel from the
voice of a narrator who tells Jack's story to the voice of the heterosexual Will
is, to say the least, surprising. But in giving direct voice to his heterosexual
rather than his gay protoganist, White invites us to consider sympathetically,
from Will's perspective, the discomfort (and even homophobia) that sometimes colors his approach to his friendship. At the same time, he brilliantly
emphasizes the ways Will's slightly alienated response to Jack and to gay
men in general reflects Jack's own early discomfort with his sexuality and his
later skeptical regard of heterosexuality. The strategy allows us to take both
men's discomforts seriously while at the same time suggesting that there is no
friendship without both mutual regard and respect of difference.

In characterizing Jack, White examines his change in understanding his
homosexuality from the early 1960s, when the novel begins, through the
1980s, when it ends. Like many of White's other novels, *Jack Holmes and
His Friend* is about a midwestern naïf who comes to New York. Initially full
of self-loathing because he accepts society's negative attitudes toward homosexuality, Jack eventually prospers sexually and emotionally, becoming, in
his own proud estimation, a "libertine" (183). This is familiar territory for
White because it expresses that same confidence in the pleasures and validity
of the flesh (and their connection to gay self-esteem) found throughout his
work. What differs is that, in writing a novel that begins in the early 1960s
and ends in the 1980s, White considers how the social context for understanding sex changes.[8] Jack lives through the closeted 1960s and the sexually permissive 1970s, articulating what he sees as the virtues of the sexual
experimentation taking place at the time over and against Will's complaints
about the constrictions of conventional married life. Ultimately, however,
Jack settles into a seemingly stable partnership in response to the AIDS
epidemic.

Also strikingly different, Jack is not, like so many of White's characters, brilliant and ambitious. He is rather average, content to live in the shadow of others, so that White seems to be exploring in *Jack Holmes* not his own life and highly original response to being gay but the life of someone perhaps more typical of the period about which he is writing. We see this most clearly, perhaps, in the Epilogue, when Jack reflects on having given up his promiscuous life in favor of a more settled one. He utters one of the most bourgeois statements about sexual morality we are ever likely to hear from one of White's major gay characters: "I must say I'm glad I changed my life. It was so empty before" (388). His statement implies that White does not intend his novel to be about revolutionary sexual change but the ways in which changing social circumstances enabled a kind of gay assimilation to American norms. Indeed, it is the straight Will who first tells Jack that it is time to change his life in response to the emergence of HIV. The triumphant defiance of *The Farewell Symphony*'s celebration of sexual freedom in the face of AIDS gives way here to something more conventional. Crucially, neither novel represents THE gay experience. Both reflect particular gay experiences, and the dialogic sense of balance in *Jack Holmes* leads White to show Will's values influencing Jack.

In its characterization of Will, the novel demonstrates how some straight men's attitudes toward homosexuality were growing and evolving along with gay men's. In this, *Jack Holmes and His Friend* finds a brilliant form for demonstrating an idea White's work often suggests but has rarely been able to demonstrate so effectively: the salutary impact gay lives and thought have had on the structure of traditional American thinking about sexuality. To understand the novel we have to, as we do with all White's works, take the attitudes and concerns of its gay characters seriously, something Will Wright learns to do more and more through his association with Jack. If the friendship between Jack and Will provides the soul of *Jack Holmes and His Friends*, however, the animating intellectual force of the novel derives from the story of Jack's marriage, his eventual infidelities, and his return to his wife.

Although Jack is in love with Will almost from the beginning, he introduces him to his friend Alex, a well-bred young New York society girl. Will himself is from a patrician Virginia family, and without filling Jack in on the details, he woos and weds Alex, which leads to a rupture in his relationship with Jack. After a chance encounter nearly a decade later, however, Will and Jack begin their friendship anew. It is the middle of the 1970s, and Jack is living a sexually free life. One of the novel's major themes emerges at this point, for the sexually uptight, traditionally moral Will finds it hard to believe when Jack tells him that his many sexual encounters and always short-lived

sexual relations are matters of choice and not a pathetic deformation of his
personality. The novel contrasts what Will calls Jack's gay role as a "lord of
misrule" (196) with his own heterosexual sense of himself as someone who
"over the years . . . learned how to curb [his] appetites and bathe every horny
move in romance" (194).

In this sense, the novel engages a serious analysis of the difference between
men who are freed from the conventions of marriage and those who are not.
If Will mistrusts Jack's sexual freedom, Jack considers that Will has been
partially "feminized" by having to please his wife within marriage (335).
However, Will comes to identify with Jack, realizing that many of the sexual
possibilities he wants in life are not dissimilar from those gay men can and
do take for granted. Will wants to take a "holiday from [his] life" (357), and
when he meets Jack's friend Pia, he begins an affair that sets him on a path
to exploring his own sexuality in some of the same open ways Jack has done.
In this recognition the novel makes its most provocative statement about the
impact of gay thought on straight self-understanding. The novel analyzes
with great subtlety differences and similarities between gay and straight lives
and assumptions, the nature of masculinity, and marriage, which, the novel
suggests, tends to repress rather than enhance sexual pleasure and knowledge. *Jack Holmes and His Friend* refuses platitudes about the superiority of
heterosexuality and marriage, and it subjects both to careful analysis within
an ethic that values sex, the body, and the pleasures that derive from both.
In this, it develops and extends White's earlier thinking about these ideas,
especially in *The Married Man*.

The novel's weakness, as might be clear already, is that it provides too
little reflection on its female characters—on Alex's efforts to respond to or
develop her own alternatives to the conventional structures of marriage the
novel brings into question or Pia's reaction to Will's often abusive emotional
treatment. White treats these characters with respect, and Alex's voice in
particular provides a wise and balanced perspective on the sometimes hys-
terical masculine posturing of both Jack and Will. But despite protesting that
she too wants a holiday from her life to match her husband's, she ultimately
plays a traditional role in taking Will back after his affairs. Pia conveniently
relocates to Italy. So, the novel resolves easily for Will, as it does for Jack, in
a rather bland normalization of desire structured around two couples who,
presumably because of AIDS, remain monogamous.

As a result, *Jack Holmes and His Friend*—which is, after all, a historical
novel—poses a profound question that can perhaps only be addressed satis-
factorily in historical hindsight: how are we to value Will's return to his marriage and Jack's acceptance of a longstanding partnership at the conclusion?

The ending of the novel suggests that both Jack and Will have retreated from the implications of the pleasures they cultivated outside the norms of conventionally structured relationships in the 1970s. Their final positions seem to deny the sexual freedoms both enjoyed and that Jack has championed throughout. One early reviewer saw the ending of White's novel as "stagey," diminishing what came before it.[9] But it might be equally valid to see this somewhat artificial conclusion as White's comment on a historically specific way of responding to the AIDS crises that emerged in the 1980s. It is not at all clear if the ending of the novel endorses its characters' choices or simply acknowledges the kinds of decisions made by many gay men at that moment in history. In *The Farewell Symphony,* White seems focused on the sexual possibilities lost to America because of AIDS. Here, his emphasis is different.

Nevertheless the ending of the novel does make clear that a profound transformation has occurred in America. It seems that Will's son Palmer is gay, and while Will himself somewhat regrets that turn of events, he is also accepting and encouraging of his son—as he ultimately is of Jack. Despite revealing something of White's typical melancholy in the analysis of sexual possibilities lost, *Jack Holmes and His Friend* also gestures toward a positive resolution of tensions between gay and straight men in America. In this, it is something of a fairy tale. But for once at least White seems to reconcile in this novel the tension between two opposing ideas that have defined his work from the beginning: the desire to be homosexual with all the difference that makes and yet still be considered normal. The understated normality of the ending of *Jack Holmes and His Friend* suggests that "the Homosexual," with his "pursed lips, dead pallor and shaped eyebrows"—the specter that haunted the narrator of *A Boy's Own Story*—has been finally laid to rest.[10] This may be the novel's most revolutionary insight—and a reminder to its readers in the twenty-first century of where gay people have been and where they have come.

Jack Holmes and His Friend is about the ways a gay man, Jack, comes to accept that his straight friend will not return his love sexually but will remain committed to him, and the ways a straight man, Will, comes to accept and respect his gay friend and even perhaps the possibilities that gay life offers his own son. It is in many ways White's most developed exploration of the theme of friendship that has run throughout his work from *A Boy's Own Story* on, and it may be true to say that the novel sees friendship as a relationship superior to others, including marriage.

CHAPTER SEVEN

Biography and Autobiography

States of Desire, Our Paris, The Flâneur,
My Lives, and *City Boy*

Although he is primarily a writer of fiction, White has become increasingly associated with two other important literary forms, biography and autobiography. This new emphasis has had an obvious effect on White's fiction, as seen in the author's experiments with writing fictional biographies and memoirs both in *Fanny* and *Hotel de Dream.* But the turn to nonfiction influences White's work in less obvious ways as well, as when White experiments (especially in *The Farewell Symphony* and his short stories) with creating characters not simply through a pattern of significant events but through their involvement in a variety of meaningful and not-so-meaningful—even trivial—ones. In many ways, White's turn to biography and autobiography seems a natural extension of the desire to write about gay people and gay experience that motivates many of his novels, with the difference being that, in the nonfiction, White speaks in his own voice as a gay man commenting on and relating to a larger intellectual culture.

Recently I sat down to talk to White about the connections between his work in autobiography and the autobiographical fictions for which he is most famous.[1] Because his comments provide an enlightening understanding of these connections, especially the impact of his biography of the French writer Jean Genet both on his fiction and nonfiction, I reproduce my interview in the appendix to this book. But one comment in particular stands out to guide our understanding of the relation of White's fiction to his autobiography. White emphasized the obvious truth that for the most part he had written his novels before he wrote his memoirs. He stated that his novels portray events in exemplary or representative terms; in contrast, his memoirs represent the realities of specific facts, people, and events even if these seem odd, unique, or possibly improbable. In making this distinction, White may seem to subscribe to a dominant critical notion distinguishing autobiography from fiction based on a pact the author makes with the reader to render his experience precisely as it happened.[2]

His comments, however, do not reject another dominant mode of thinking that stresses similarities between autobiography and fiction: "[Autobiography] is unquestionably a document about a life. . . . But it is also a work of art, and the literary devotee . . . will be aware of its stylistic harmony and the beauty of its images."[3] That is, White does not deny that his novels contain autobiographical elements or that his memoirs and autobiography are artfully arranged with all the tools available to him as a literary craftsman. But he does suggest that autobiography frees him to concentrate on the specific, even odd things that have actually happened to him without following the representative logic of fiction. What is more, it allows him to state directly what he thinks. We might explore, then, some of the ways the two genres create a vibrant dialogue with one another. It would be a mistake to look to the autobiographies for the "truth" behind White's fictions—for, as he suggests, fiction creates its own truth. But the ideas the author reveals in his autobiographies (and even in his biographies) often help us understand the complexity of thought in White's fiction and see better how he constructs fiction to make his ideas perspicuous to the reader.

Even though, as Paul Robinson shows, gay autobiography proliferated in America from the 1970s onward,[4] White's first genuine memoirs were delayed until he had written the autobiographical novels that made him famous. More interestingly, they did not appear until he had proven himself the master of another form altogether—biography. In 1993, White published a life of the French novelist and playwright Jean Genet that earned the author not only the National Book Critics Circle Award but one of the French government's most prestigious awards in literature and the arts, the *Chevalier de L'Ordre des Arts et des Lettres*. According to White, the experience of writing this biography significantly affected his subsequent work, most obviously, perhaps, by preparing him to write about two other major French authors, *Marcel Proust* (1999) and (Arthur) *Rimbaud: The Double Life of a Rebel* (2008).

Because all three writers are important to a modern history of homosexuality, White's biographies form something of a continuum with the thematic exploration of sexuality in his other works. One signal achievement of White's biography of Genet is that it placed "Genet's personal and literary vision squarely in his exclusively homosexual experience" at a time when homosexuality was still not honestly explored in criticism or the literary classroom.[5] The same is true of White's biography of Proust, which emphasizes the impact his homosexuality had on his great sequence of novels, *In Search of Lost Time*. White's biographies provide valuable clues to his own interests as well, for all three writers influenced White significantly. White's narrator in *A Boy's Own Story*, for example, makes repeated reference to the young poet Rimbaud's harsh treatment of the older Verlaine as a model for the kind of adult sexual power he wishes to wield over another man. Or, to take another example, Genet's figure of the homosexual as a sexual outlaw provides one of the few positive experiences of homosexuality the young narrator of *The Beautiful Room Is Empty* feels. And, finally, Proust's concern with involuntary memory provides insight into White's thematizing memory in *Forgetting Elena* and all his autobiographical novels. White's choice of subjects for his biographies provides, then, opportunities to explore some of the most significant literary influences on his own fiction, so they seem highly personal works. Not surprisingly, writing these biographies encouraged White to think about his fiction in new ways.

White has so far produced at least three autobiographical works: *Our Paris: Sketches from Memory* (1994), *My Lives: An Autobiography* (2005), and *City Boy: My Life in New York During the 1960s and '70s* (2009). For the sake of precision, we might think of *Our Paris* and *City Boy* as memoirs, for like that form they tend to emphasize everyday events and particular people important in the life of the author. *My Lives* seems to be more a genuine autobiography (as White himself styles it in the original hardcover printing of the book), for it has a greater degree of the self-reflexive concern for understanding the whole meaning of its author's life that characterizes formal autobiography. Nevertheless all three works actually blend autobiography and memoir in ways Bertram Cohler sees as characteristic of the genre, gay "life writing," in the postwar era in the United States.[6] Two other works, *States of Desire: Travels in Gay America* (1980) and *The Flâneur: A Stroll Through the Paradoxes of Paris* (2001) are not, strictly speaking, memoir or autobiography. Yet both usefully document elements of White's life and thought at different periods in his creative life. So, both merit discussion, however brief, in this context.

White's most intimate memoir, *Our Paris: Sketches from Memory* speaks about the author's life with Hubert Sorin, the young man who became White's lover and partner in the late 1980s in Paris, and whose harrowing death from AIDS just five years after they met provided the inspiration for the characters of Brice in *The Farewell Symphony* and Julien in *The Married*

Man. The lightness of touch in *Our Paris*—a book that records the everyday, trivial incidents in White's and Sorin's lives in the early 1990s—seems crucial to the work, which evokes two lives in the process of being lived without a great deal of regard for the death of Sorin. Although White says in the interview below he knows it is coming, Sorin's death, in fact, is the subject only of the introduction of the book (where White says that he wrote these little sketches to provide context for the often harshly satirical pen-and-ink drawings Sorin completed toward the end of his life) and its afterword. Sorin was an architect by training, and his illness kept him from working. But in his last months, his creative vision was channeled through drawings that achieved a modicum of success in the Paris art world and in the book he produced with White.

My Lives takes up the significant people, issues, and events in White's life, and provides as full a picture as White himself has yet given of his personal relationships. In this, it is a singularly important source of information about the author. Still, *My Lives* is organized around a series of themes or topics. Individual chapters range from the bland "My Mother" (the topic of which is obvious) through more provocative titles such as "My Women" (which concerns White's closest female friends), "My Master" (about his masochistic love for a much younger man), and "My Blonds" (detailing his important lovers over the years). In the interview below White explains the essayistic structure of *My Lives* as a way of creating an autobiography that did not have to begin with his childhood, which he felt he had written enough about already. But rather than simply reveal the facts of White's life, *My Lives* records the author's ideas about those facts, and thus gives particular meaning to them. Edmund White, the subject of *My Lives*, is not simply a man who has lived an extraordinary life, but one in the process of thinking about what that life has meant.

Finally, *City Boy* is a fascinating exploration of New York in the 1960s and 1970s, in what was surely a high point in the city's recent intellectual history. The book reveals something about White often remarked: his great gift for friendship. If White's young fictional narrators constantly seek the affirmations of friendship, it is perhaps because the adult writer knows well the value of attaining them. In *City Boy*, White explores his intimate acquaintance not only with the major gay artists and intellectuals of the period— Michel Foucault, Thom Gunn, Robert Mapplethorpe, for instance—but with an entire generation of public figures. The book is not quite chronological in outline, but structured more traditionally than his other works around the author's arrival in New York and his coming to meet the important people he knew. Because many of these people died of AIDS in the 1980s, the memoir is an important, highly personal record of their lives. It seems useful for understanding the social context of White's early novels, and gives a sense of who White may have imagined his readers to be in a time before there was a clearly established readership for gay novels in America. While this memoir doesn't provide a great deal of information to help White's readers understand his early autobiographical novels, it provides intriguing insight into the intellectual milieu White satirized in *Caracole* and eulogized in *The Farewell Symphony*. Its great achievement is to show how the mainstreaming of gay lives that began to take place in America in the 1990s had its genesis in the strong intellectual thought of the 1960s and 1970s.

I mention *States of Desire* and *The Flâneur* in this context because both reveal a dimension of White's life and thought easily overlooked, the way gay identity in White's work—no matter how one understands that vexed concept—is always conceived and contextualized in particular times and places. In *States of Desire,* White incorporates personal, autobiographical elements into what is essentially a nonfiction account of gay life in 1970s America. His exploration of American subcultural communities of gay men in the era before AIDS is, therefore, a significant source of knowledge about White before he was a famous author. In a real sense, this early gay travelogue becomes something of a portrait of the artist as a young gay man, and White's narrative embrace of the gay communities he discovers across America reveals something about the ways both he and a generation of middle-class, gay white men came of age in the 1970s.

Like *States of Desire, The Flâneur* is more travelogue than memoir, for its primary subject is not White himself but Paris. Still, it explores Paris through White's eyes, and thus reveals White in his association with Paris. The conceit of the book also betrays its relationship to *Our Paris,* with that book's emphasis on the idiosyncratic joys of life in the French capital. A *flâneur,* White explains, is someone who strolls aimlessly about the city, watching and reacting to urban delights that reveal themselves seemingly by chance. White, the narrator of *The Flâneur,* experiences by happenstance what he would not have imagined beforehand, and reveals himself, or even grows, in accordance with his seemingly random experiences. It is a more relaxed way of presenting oneself than we are perhaps used to in White's highly analytical novels, but like the novels it doesn't retreat from the implication that one creates oneself out of experience. Underlying this work is the assurance that the Paris he reveals to us is the Paris already important to him, the Paris he has sought out to construct himself in a particular way. It is the Paris of artists and intellectuals, and if White celebrates the random and even sometimes trivial aspects of this Paris, the book is a portrait of the artist in firm command of his person and persona as an important figure schooling his reader in the best the city has to offer.

All these autobiographical nonfictions exhibit White's virtuoso habit as a novelist of creating new formal structures to represent their subject, in this case White himself. Each is, in its own right, something of a masterpiece of literary style. Consequently, rather than comfortably reassuring us about the distinctions between fact and fiction, autobiography and novel, they remind us of a theme throughout White's fiction: the possibility of re-imagining one's life anew, in a different way, and the utility of art and writing in the pursuit of such imagining. As Roland Barthes suggests, autobiography is less an imitation or description of the life one has lived than a way of nominating or signifying that life,[7] calling it into existence in a particular way. Real life, too, can be subjected to imaginative reinscription. To read the autobiographies, then, provides clues not simply to the "facts" behind White's "fictions" but the techniques and habits of mind that shape his particular visions of the world.

Reading *States of Desire*, for instance, we perhaps discover if not a source then an analogue for White's remarkable sociological imagination in the early autobiographical novels. The discerning, critical eye he casts on the gay lives emerging in 1970s America reminds us of the distance White maintains from the social processes through which gay subcultural communities were constructed in all his works. But such discernment does not forestall White's immensely sympathetic understanding of the ways gay men constructed identities and communities for themselves in a society that routinely disparaged them. He remains always aware of both the pleasures and pitfalls of those constructions. *States of Desire* thus reveals something about the double-narrative voice that characterizes White's novels. If White writes sympathetically about his fictional narrators' struggles within social forces that distort their happiness, another voice in the novels replicates the sociological awareness that it is only once they refashion themselves in their own ways that they will achieve the kinds of personal and communal strengths celebrated in *States of Desire*. This early work—part sociological tract, part biography of an emerging community, and part autobiography—reveals a confluence of ideas in White's work that helps explain his early fiction as well as any critical evaluation might. It suggests why White's novels reveal his gay characters in the curiously fractured ways they do—boys and men who at their best scrutinize and re-invent themselves and at their worst calcify into distorted figures impervious to the constant flux of social change.

Read side-by-side with the novels, *Our Paris* points toward the significance of White's differential shaping of *The Farewell Symphony*, which tells a story of living bracketed by death, and *The Married Man,* which reveals a process of dying. Brice's death from AIDs is one the narrator of *The Fare-well Symphony* says he cannot finish telling, while White writes of Julien's death in *The Married Man* only in the third person. In their own ways, then, both novels suggest that death from AIDS is a story the autobiographical voice, even a fictional one, cannot or should not have to tell, which may also explain why Sorin's death is not fundamental to *Our Paris.* Ironically, the story may be too personal.[8]

It seems significant that White has never produced another nonfictional portrayal of his lover's life and death outside this small work. He even largely passes over Sorin in *My Lives,* which covers a great deal of White's life in Paris. The silence corroborates the reticence on the part of the narrator to speak about the death of one so close to him that we see in *The Farewell Symphony.* Its suggests, too, that White is aware of the ways his fictional portrayals of Brice and Julien have to stand representatively for a truth about the horrors AIDS brought onto a generation of gay men, a truth more profound than the facts of any single life can suggest. And yet, the charm of *Our Paris*—evoked through its record of the eccentric joys in living of White and his partner—testifies as well to the persistence of the pleasures of day-to-day life that even AIDS cannot erase. It reminds us that the novels do not simply record but embody the loss of such stories and the lives they reflect. White's novels about Sorin are elegies, and like other types of that form they signal by their absence the life and vivacity that attends the death of vigorous young men. *Our Paris,* a memoir of living, reclaims both, and so somehow seems essential to the whole story White sets out to tell.

Finally, *My Lives,* with its even-handed but often harsh judgment of the people in White's life (especially his parents), provides a renewed appreciation for how carefully White works in his fiction to create empathy with characters who were not always, in real life, sympathetic. If the portrait of White's father that emerges in his fiction is that of a distant man, he is also the locus of desire that gives shape to the narrator's self-understanding. But in *My Lives* White reveals him as much more competitive and cold than he is portrayed in the novels. The young White himself is shown to be much more promiscuous, and much more intelligent, than the boy in White's novels, so that it becomes clear how White negotiates his readers' willingness (or lack thereof) to indulge the sexual themes of his novels.

My Lives tells us, too, of White's idealizing intellect, of how he transforms realities into ideas implying something greater. So, in the chapter titled "My Blonds," the reader discovers that Jim Ruddy, the figure White has written about as Sean, the great love of the narrator's life in *The Beautiful*

Room Is Empty, is someone that White did not know all that well. The idea of Jim Ruddy, what he represented in terms of love and desire for the young writer, is more important than the man himself. If we consider that White often talks about the man Jim Ruddy and the character Sean in the very same terms, we might conclude the truth of this point both for White's fiction and his autobiography. And we might see better that, although fiction and autobiography are two different genres, they can often explore similar ideas and related truths.

In the interview below White explains the essayistic structure of *My Lives* as a way of creating an autobiography that did not have to begin in childhood, which he felt he had written enough about already. Still, this fascinating formal conceit opens itself to other interpretations. When the narrators of White's autobiographical novels say they feel as if they inhabit multiple selves, they may be repeating something the author himself feels as he records his own life in a series of essays shaped as an attempt to understand or possess himself through different types or styles of relationships.

The chapters of the book are all developed around the conceit of the author's relation to individuals or groups: White writes about "My Women," "My Master," and "My Blonds." We might question the nature of the "me" who can possess his "master," and his relationship to the "me" who can possess his "women" and "blonds." Two notions of possession (and self-possession) do not add up to a coherent whole. So rather than clarify a relationship among the seemingly competing notions of sex, love, and friendship to be found in White's novels, *My Lives* seems to confirm their separation, even as it idealizes each. And rather than settle the question of identity in White's work, the autobiography simply confirms its ambiguity and multiplicity. On the one hand, the autobiography suggests that, even in considering the facts of his life, White does not reduce them to the consistencies of that Enlightenment convention, a single self. On the other hand, however, the repetitive insistence of the word *my* seems to insist on a consistent single self, so we understand the autobiography point to an Enlightenment convention by which an author imposes a coherent form and understanding to the subject he knows as "myself."

APPENDIX

Interview: Edmund White on Biography, Autobiography, and Fiction

Nicholas F. Radel: Beginning with *Sketches from Memory* and *The Flâneur,* the personal narrative or memoir begins to take shape as something of a sub-genre in your work. Was there something in those books . . . that you couldn't quite express in your novels at the time?

Edmund White: I think it was what I might have thought of as slightly trivial aspects of everyday lives . . . the freaky little things that would happen to you, when you would lean out the window and hear a girl singing and then that would turn out to be something. Or just the interchange with the shopkeepers which you know plays such a huge role in your daily life but doesn't seem worthy of writing about. I think because Hubert [Sorin] liked to draw that sort of thing, and he was good at it, that I permitted myself to write about those things that normally I might have been too snobbish to write about.

NR: And yet *The Flâneur* is not really about trivial things, but something more substantial. It's a stroll taken through the city much as Baudelaire might have done, glimpsing its meaning and mystery in a highly personal way.

EW: The idea of ambling through the city with no purpose but coming back with a haul at the end of every day almost willy-nilly appealed to me . . . although I think I'm still too puritanical and purpose-driven to really be a *flâneur.* . . .

NR: Did your experience writing *Sketches from Memory* and *The Flâneur* motivate your decision later to write autobiography and memoir in *City Boy* and *My Lives*? Was there a conscious connection?

EW: I think only in the sense that I was surprised at how interested people were even in these trivial facts of everyday life, so it kind of gave me the courage to go into great detail in those two later books. But I think the really important influence in my career was the Genet biography, because I think that writing a biography where you start at the beginning of somebody's life and go to the end, and you take the most disparate events and you just tack them all onto this name, Jean Genet, and you say, well, I can swear to you he really did all these things, and he's one man moving through time and I'm going to start from the beginning and go to the end. It's going to be strictly chronological, and I'm going to tell you all the things he did. I mean that he was dancing in his nightgown for the Black Panthers . . . that he was a tough guy and that he was the friend of various heads of state, that he was a friend of the Palestinians, and that when he started out he was a peasant boy in the Morvan and never went to school beyond age twelve. It is such an unlikely story, [because] he wasn't a primitive writer who might have emerged from such a background. He was one of the most sophisticated writers France ever produced. So I think that I was so impressed by the fact that you could attach all these events to a single name and float him through time and get people to believe it and that it had a kind of plausibility made me more courageous in the inclusiveness of especially *The Farewell Symphony*. Because I think before that with *Boy's Own Story* and *The Beautiful Room Is Empty,* I'd been very concerned about making a shapely story, so that it seemed to have a beginning, middle, and an end. Although neither of those books is especially well constructed, nevertheless there's a kind of coherence and you feel that an awful lot is being left out and that only certain things are being dwelled on, and those rather intensely. Whereas by the time I get to *Farewell Symphony* . . . partly it's the exigencies of writing such a book because I decided to collapse volumes three and four into one book, so the '70s and the '80s all had to come into one book. . . . But because I had written *Genet* I felt like you could just cram so many different items into this one reticule. . . .

NR: So, you're suggesting that *The Farewell Symphony* and *The Married Man,* which were both being written around this time, proceeded from a different sense of how you were going to shape your fictional experience.

EW: Yes. Those two novels are filtered through memory and elegy, I think, whereas I don't think you can say that about *Our Paris* or *The Flâneur.* Yes, of course, there's always the knowledge that Hubert is sick and dying in *Our Paris,* but that's held at bay pretty much, and there's a kind of cheerful gallantry about these books that's absent from those bigger works.

NR: You said earlier too that you thought the experience of writing *Genet* really led you to work and think about memoir and autobiography. . . .

EW: Well, it was capacious, you know. I mean in other words the biography of Genet was the most capacious work I'd ever written where I followed somebody for eighty-six years of his life. And it felt to me like he had had many different lives, and yet they all kind of, they all happened to the same person. So, there's some continuity, and he definitely had a very strong personality, much stronger than mine. So, you know, I think that's what impressed me as a model, as a literary model.

NR: Did this sense that Genet had many different lives influence your decision to write *My Lives* as a series of topics focused on your relationships with other people?

EW: Well, I had read Gorky's books called *My Childhood* and *My Universities,* and then Verlaine had written a book called *My Prisons.* . . . Anyway, I thought, I find childhood boring, and I've written about it a lot already, and I don't really want to rehash all that. And I thought if I write by topics, then I'll be obliged to write essays, really. And if you write an essay, you have to have a point of view and a conclusion. I mean in other words, I'd written so much in fiction about going to shrinks, but I'd never really said what I thought about it. Do I approve, disapprove? Think it was worth it, not worth it? Some are better than others, you know. So, I thought, well, if I write a chapter called "My Shrinks," I'll have to at least end with three or four pages where I say something about the whole phenomenon. And I think by nature I tend to avoid that kind of drawing conclusions. I don't really like it. If I'm looking at it from a positive point of view, I'd say I'm a born novelist in the sense that I like to dramatize interesting situations without necessarily taking a point of view, and because I don't really always know what my point of view would be. But still I thought well this is good because if I write about "My Women," then I'll have to say what I really think about women. Do I wish they would just go away, or do I really love them or what? I think I also thought that we live in such a politically correct period that it would be quite sort of daring and shocking to have to reconsider all these essential things from the ground up and say what you actually thought.

NR: So, I was going to ask if the writing of *Genet* and your interest in autobiography in some ways explains the turn toward historical fiction in your work as well. *Fanny* and *Hotel de Dream* were written during the same time period as *City Boy* and *My Lives.* Is there a relationship between them? What explains your seemingly new interest in historical fiction?

EW: Well, I think that partly it's a flight from "I." In other words, you know, if you're writing so much stuff about yourself, you get fed up with that and you want . . . to enact your own dramas in other terms. In other words you want to be other people, and you'll see that this novel I've just finished [*Jack Holmes and His Friend* (2012)] goes yet another step because the two main characters, the straight guy and the gay guy, don't really resemble me in any way. . . . I got this idea from Nabokov's book, *Look at the Harlequins!*, that you could take a kind of caricature of yourself and put him out in the world. In other words [some] people think [after reading *Lolita*] that Nabokov himself must have been a nympholept. And . . . so in *Look at the Harlequins!*, he creates a character who is a kind of drooling, dirty old man and who is a Russian aristocrat. . . . So I thought, well that would be funny . . . to try to play on my public image, [although] it's not a very strong one. . . . But what I tried to do was to give a character somewhat the trajectory of my life, going to the University of Michigan, coming to New York in '62, working for a big magazine and so on, but have him be an entirely different person completely—gay, but very good looking, completely unambitious, you know, kind of upper middle classed, reserved, all these things I'm not. . . . And so, it's kind of historical fiction in the sense that it's about the '60s and '70s; it's kind of autobiographical in that the character follows the same trajectory I did. But it's also imaginative in that the character is entirely different, and what he makes of his situation in life is quite different from what I made of mine.

NR: So, does that difference between fact and fiction provide a general model for your work? Would you say it describes the relationship between your autobiographies and your autobiographical fictions?

EW: Well, I think usually the fictional version precedes the actual autobiography. I don't try to play around in merging the two genres. I hate that. And I can't bear it when people talk about creative nonfiction. That sounds like lying to me. And so I don't try to play with levels of reality and so on. . . . When I write a novel, I can completely re-create the sensual and emotional surround without awakening any plausibility doubts. In other words, I can say that the boy in *A Boy's Own Story* is on the dock, and he's watching a tiny ant crawl up his arm that looks like a dumbbell. Well, he was like sixteen and I'm writing this at age forty-six. You know, it's very unlikely that thirty years later I'd remember an ant. But I don't think that question comes up because it is a novel, and it's called a novel. . . . In a novel you have an obligation to be representative. If you're showing a gay character you should show a representative gay character. Not a total marginal freak, but somebody who is sort of average looking, and maybe average to slightly better than average abilities, average to slightly better than average curiosity about the world. Strange parents, but not impossibly weird and so on. Whereas when I came to write *My Lives*, I thought, OK, I've done that. Now I'm writing an autobiography, and I'm saying "this really happened," so I can dare to put in all the bizarre things that really happened to me. Because I think if your obligation in a novel is to be representative, your only obligation in an autobiography is to be truthful.

NOTES

Chapter One—Understanding Edmund White

1. Edmund White, *The Beautiful Room Is Empty* (New York: Random House, 1988), 226. Subsequent references will be cited in the text.

2. Christopher Bram, *Eminent Outlaws: The Gay Writers Who Changed America* (New York: Twelve, 2012), ix.

3. David Leavitt, Introduction to Keith Fleming, *Original Youth: The Real Story of Edmund White's Boyhood* (Green Candy Press, 2003), xxi.

4. Jerry W. Carlson, "Edmund White's Brilliant New Novel of Sexual Awakening," review of *A Boy's Own Story, Book Week, Chicago Sun-Times*, 26 September 1982, 27.

5. Christopher Lehmann-Haupt, review of *A Boy's Own Story, New York Times*, 17 December 1982, C37.

6. Fleming, *Original Youth*, 1.

7. Ibid, 75.

8. Stephen Barber, *Edmund White: The Burning World* (New York: St. Martin's Press, 1999), 23.

9. *Dark Currents* exists in typescript and manuscript in the Edmund White Papers, Yale Collection of American Literature, Beinecke Rare Book and Manuscript Library, Uncat. ZA, MS. 240, Box 8, Acquired July 1991; another copy, retitled *The Tower Window*, can be found in the same collection (Box 18). White discusses the novel in *My Lives: An Autobiography* (New York: Ecco, 2006), 264.

10. David Bergman, *The Violet Hour: The Violet Quill and the Making of Gay Culture* (New York: Columbia University Press, 2004), 121. *The Blue Boy in Black* exists in typescript in the Edmund White Papers, Yale Collection of American Literature, Beinecke Rare Book and Manuscript Library, Uncat. ZA, MS. 240, Box 5, Acquired July 1991.

11. White's novel is not to be confused with Felice Picano's 1995 novel of the same name. Picano apparently appropriated a title he thought White had abandoned (unpublished interview with author, 5 August 2011).

12. Alan Friedman, review of *Forgetting Elena, New York Times Book Review*, 25 March 1973, 3.

13. Robert McRuer, *The Queer Renaissance: Contemporary American Literature and the Reinvention of Lesbian and Gay Identities* (New York: New York University Press, 1997), 1.

14. Edmund White, "Out of the Closet, on to the Bookshelf," in *The Burning Library*, ed. David Bergman (New York: Alfred A. Knopf, 1994), 280.

15. Richard Goldstein, "Modus Eroticus," review of *States of Desire, Village Voice,* 28 January 1980, 41. See also Jerry Phillips, who defines White's work within a "motive of discovery" in classical travel writing that seeks to "record for the first time a people or land unknown to the traveler's world" (181) ("Into the Melting Pot: Utopian and Dystopian Themes in Edmund White's *Travels in Gay America*," *Studies in Travel Writing* 1.1 [Spring 1997]: 170–98).

16. Felice Picano, "Edmund White and the Violet Quill Club," *Review of Contemporary Fiction* 16.3 (Fall 1996): 85.

17. Bergman, *The Violet Hour,* 61; Bergman summarizes and quotes from Robert Ferro, "Gay Literature Today," in *The Violet Quill Reader: The Emergence of Gay Writing after Stonewall,* ed. David Bergman (New York: St. Martin's 1994), 391.

18. Barber, *Edmund White,* 95.

19. Edmund White, *City Boy: My Life in New York During the 1960s and '70s* (New York: Bloomsbury, 2009), 185.

20. Kay Bonetti, "An Interview with Edmund White," *Missouri Review* 13.2 (Summer 1990): 97.

21. Thomas C. Spear, "Edmund White on Queer Autofiction, Biography, and Sidafiction," *a/b: Auto/Biography Studies* 15.2 (Winter 2000): 267.

22. Tony Purvis, "America's 'White' Cultural and Sexual Dissensus: The Fictions of Edmund White," *Journal of American Studies* 42.2 (2008): 294.

23. In addition to *The Blue Boy in Black* and *Terre Haute,* White has also had one other play produced. An unpublished drama, *Trios,* explores parallels in the erotic triangles of people from three different historical periods and social classes. Apparently written in the late 1970s or early 1980s, *Trios* was staged at the Haymarket Theatre, Leicester, in 1990, the Riverside Studios, Hammersmith, London, in 1993, and the Granary Theatre, Cork, Ireland in 1995. *Trios* can be found under its original title, *Three Times Three,* as a photocopied typescript in the Edmund White Papers, Yale Collection of American Literature, Beinecke Rare Book and Manuscript Library, Uncat. ZA, MS. 240, Box 17, Acquired July 1991.

24. Bergman, *The Violet Hour,* 50. "Sad young men" was the title of a popular song of the sixties, cited by another gay critic, Richard Dyer, to describe this literature in *The Matter of Images: Essays on Representation* (London: Routledge, 1993).

25. Bergman, *The Violet Hour,* 59.

26. Bonetti, "An Interview with Edmund White," 101.

27. See Les Brookes, *Gay Male Fiction Since Stonewall: Ideology, Conflict, and Aesthetics* (New York: Routledge, 2009), 75–76.

28. Nicholas F. Radel, "Self as Other: The Politics of Identity in the Works of Edmund White," in *Queer Words, Queer Images: Communication and the Construction of Homosexuality,* ed. R. Jeffrey Ringer (New York: New York University Press, 1994), 176.

29. McRuer, *The Queer Renaissance,* 36.

30. Bergman, *The Violet Hour,* 72.

31. Purvis, "America's 'White' Cultural and Sexual Dissensus," 306.

32. Nicholas F. Radel, "(E)racing Edmund White: Queer Reading, Race, and Sexuality in *A Boy's Own Story,*" *Modern Fiction Studies* 54.4 (Winter 2008): 767.

33. Brookes, *Gay Male Fiction,* 16.

Chapter Two—White's Autobiographical Trilogy

1. Edmund White, *The Farewell Symphony* (New York: Alfred A. Knopf, 1997), 40. Subsequent references will be cited in the text.

2. See Ed Cohen, "Constructing Gender," in *The Columbia History of the American Novel,* ed. Emory Elliott, Cathy Davidson, Patrick O'Donnell, Valerie Smith, and Christopher Wilson (New York: Columbia University Press, 1991), 552.

3. Edmund White, "The Personal Is Political," in *The Burning Library,* ed. Bergman, 372.

4. On the ways the novel resists the conventions of the "coming-out novel," see Nicholas F. Radel, "Edmund White," in *Dictionary of Literary Biography: American Novelists Since World War II,* 6th series, ed. James and Wanda Giles (Columbia, S.C.: Bruccoli, Clark, Layman, Inc., 2000), 343. For a more complete analysis of the failure of coming-out as a liberatory strategy in gay literature in reference to *A Boy's Own Story,* see Angus Gordon, "The Retrospective Closet: Adolescence and Queer Prehistory," *Australian Historical Studies* 36.126 (October 2005): 315–31.

5. Edmund White, "The Personal Is Political," 372.

6. Christopher Lehmann-Haupt, "Edmund White's Tale of a Gay Youth," review of *The Beautiful Room Is Empty, New York Times,* 17 March 1988, C29.

7. Edmund White, "The Personal Is Political," 372.

8. Radel, "Self as Other," 181.

9. Edmund White, *A Boy's Own Story* (New York: New American Library, 1983), 213. Subsequent references will be cited in the text.

10. Purvis, "America's 'White' Cultural and Sexual Dissensus," 303.

11. Eve Kosofsky Sedgwick, *Between Men: English Literature and Male Homosocial Desire* (New York: Columbia University Press, 1985), 1–2.

12. See McRuer, *The Queer Renaissance,* 40ff, as well as the response to McRuer by Radel, "(E)racing Edmund White," 766–90.

13. White, *The Beautiful Room Is Empty,* 227. Subsequent references will be cited in the text.

14. Alan Hollinghurst, "A Prince of Self Approval," in *Times Literary Supplement,* 19 August 1983, 875; but see the correction by Radel, "Self as Other," 192n3.

15. George Stambolian, Introduction to *Men on Men: Best New Gay Fiction* (New York: New American Library, 1986), 8.

16. John Rechy, "Together They Stood," review of *The Beautiful Room Is Empty, Washington Post Book World,* April 3, 1988, 4.

17. Stephen Adams, *The Homosexual as Hero in Contemporary Fiction* (London: Vision Press Ltd., 1980), 183.

18. Purvis, "America's 'White' Dissensus," 294.

19. Wilfrid R. Koponen provides a usefully detailed discussion of the narrator's encounter with psychoanalysis in *Embracing a Gay Identity: Gay Novels as Guides* (Westport, Conn.: Bergin & Garvey, 1993), 73–98.

20. Reed Woodhouse, *Unlimited Embrace: A Canon of Gay Fiction, 1945–1995* (Amherst: University of Massachusetts Press, 1998), 291, 293.

21. Barber, *Edmund White,* 107.

22. Purvis, "America's 'White' Dissensus," 306.

23. Edmund White, *States of Desire: Travels in Gay America* (New York: Dutton, 1980), 282.

24. Larry Kramer, "Sex and Sensibility," *Advocate* 734 (27 May 1997): 59. For an analysis of Larry Kramer's responses to AIDS, see David Bergman, "Larry Kramer and the Rhetoric of AIDS," in *Gaiety Transfigured: Gay Self Representation in American Literature.* (Madison: University of Wisconsin Press, 1991), 122–38.

25. Edmund White, "The Joy of Gay Lit," *Out* (September 1997): 197.

Chapter Three — AIDS Fiction

1. Bonetti, "An Interview with Edmund White," 97.

2. Peter Christensen, "'A More Angular and Less Predictable Way': Epiphanies in Edmund White's *The Darker Proof*," *Review of Contemporary Fiction* 16.3 (1996): 75.

3. John M. Clum, "'And Once I Had It All': AIDS Narratives and Memories of an American Dream," in *Writing AIDS: Gay Literature, Language, and Analysis*, ed. Timothy F. Murphy and Suzanne Poirier (New York: Columbia University Press, 1993), 201. Clum's essay usefully surveys early literary and cinematic responses to AIDS.

4. Larry Kramer, "A Personal Appeal," *New York Native* (24 August–6 September 1981), rpt. in *Reports from the Holocaust: The Making of an AIDS Activist* (New York: St. Martin's, 1989), 8.

5. Bergman, "Larry Kramer and the Rhetoric of AIDS," 125.

6. Patrick Buchanan, *New York Post*, 26 June 1991; qtd. in Lee Edelman, "The Mirror and the Tank: 'AIDS,' Subjectivity, and the Rhetoric of Activism, in *Writing AIDS*, ed. Murphy and Poirier, 24.

7. Brookes, *Gay Male Fiction*, 176.

8. Susan Sontag, *AIDS and Its Metaphors* (New York: Farrar, Straus, and Giroux, 1989), 72.

9. Edmund White and Adam Mars-Jones, *The Darker Proof: Stories from a Crisis* (New York: New American Library, 1988), 213-14. Subsequent references to stories in this, the American edition of this collection, will be cited in the text.

10. Richard Dellamora, "Apocalyptic Utterance in Edmund White's 'An Oracle,'" in *Writing AIDS*, ed. Murphy and Poirier, 113; see also Robert D. Fulk, "Greece and Homosexual Identity in Edmund White's 'An Oracle,'" *College Literature* 24.1 (February 1997): 227–39, who reads in the story Ray's "search for a new identity and a mature sexual role" (234).

11. Richard Dellamora, "Apocalyptic Utterance," 114.

12. Brookes, *Gay Male Fiction*, 179.

13. Stephen Barber provides details about the stories' publication history as well as a chronology: "Skinned Alive" (1989), "Reprise" (1992), "His Biographer" (March 1994), "Watermarked," "Pyrography," and "Cinnamon Skin" (later in 1994 following the death of Hubert Sorin) (*Edmund White*, 260–63).

14. Edmund White, *Skinned Alive: Stories* (New York: Vintage International, 1995), 225. Subsequent references to the stories in the paperback edition will be cited in the text.

15. Christensen, "'A More Angular and Less Predictable Way,'" 80.

16. Raymond-Jean Frontain, "Ardor with a Silent H: Submitting to the Ache of Love in Edmund White's 'Skinned Alive,'" in *The Postmodern Short Story: Forms and*

NOTES TO PAGES 50-72

Issues, ed. Farhat Iftekharrudin, Joseph Boyden, Mary Rohrberger, and Jaie Claudet (Westport, Conn.: Praeger, 2003), 155.

17. Ibid., 141.

18. White, *The Farewell Symphony*, 413. Subsequent references will be cited in the text.

19. Purvis, America's 'White' Cultural and Sexual Dissensus," 312.

20. Brookes, *Gay Male Fiction*, 162.

21. Edmund White, *The Married Man* (New York: Vintage Books, 2000), 59. Subsequent references will be cited in the text.

22. White, *States of Desire*, 282.

23. James Hopkins, "Degeneration Games," review of *The Married Man*, *Guardian*, 24 March 2000, http://www.guardian.co.uk/books/2000/mar/25/fiction.reviews1? INTCMP=SRCHDegeneration games.

Chapter Four—Early Experimental Fiction

1. On the difficulties of getting the work into print, see White, *City Boy*, 59-60. Subsequent references will be cited in the text.

2. Bergman, *The Violet Hour*, 149.

3. Ibid.; for a full history of the association of the setting of *Forgetting Elena* with Fire Island, see Chris A. Lovell, "Remembering Elena: A Review of Criticism of Edmund White's First Published Novel," *Harrington Gay Men's Literary Quarterly* 8.1 (2006): 119–31.

4. Edmund White, *Forgetting Elena* (New York: Random House, 1973; rpt. New York: Penguin Books, 1981), 83. Subsequent references will be cited in the text.

5. Harry Mathews, "A Valentine for Elena," *Review of Contemporary Fiction* 16.3 (Fall 1996): 35. White himself makes similar points, see Bonetti, "An Interview with Edmund White," 102.

6. Brookes, *Gay Male Fiction*, 78.

7. Ibid.

8. Larry McCaffery and Sinda Gregory, *Alive and Writing: Interviews with American Authors of the 1980s* (Urbana: University of Illinois Press, 1987), 260; "Edmund White Speaks with Edmund White," *Review of Contemporary Fiction* 16.3 (Fall 1996): 15.

9. See Lovell, "Remembering Elena," 129ff.

10. White, "Edmund White Speaks," 15.

11. Barber, *Edmund White*, 51; Bergman, *The Violet Hour*, 147.

12. Brookes, *Gay Male Fiction*, 93.

13. J. D. McClatchy, "Baroque Inventions," *Shenandoah* 30.1 (Fall 1978): 97–98.

14. For a different reading of Elena's authenticity, see Brookes, *Gay Male Fiction*, 80.

15. Jacques Lacan, "The Mirror Stage as Formative of the Function of the I as Revealed in Psychoanalytic Experience," in *Écrits: A Selection*, trans. Alan Sheridan (New York: W. W. Norton, 1977), 2.

16. White, *My Lives*, 27.

17. Mathews, "A Valentine," 36.

18. Edmund White, *Nocturnes for the King of Naples* (New York: St. Martin's Press, 1978; rpt. New York: Penguin Books, 1980), 32. Subsequent references will be cited in the text.

19. Bergman, *Gaiety Transfigured,* 196; for an elaboration of the novel's connections to *A Boy's Own Story,* see Radel, "Self as Other," 187ff.

20. Bergman, *Gaiety Transfigured,* 196.

21. Ibid.

22. McClatchy, "Baroque Inventions," 97.

23. Neil Bartlett, "The Uses of Monotony: Repetition in the Language of Oscar Wilde, Jean Genet, Edmund White and Juan Goytisolo," in *Flowers and Revolution: A Collection of Writings on Jean Genet,* ed. Barbara Read with Ian Birchall (London: Middlesex University Press, 1997), 123.

24. On the masturbatory qualities of White's prose, and the narrator's self-seduction, see Bartlett, "The Uses of Monotony,"126.

25. On the novel as a dialogue of "self and soul," the narrator's address to his own past self, or even the narrator's artistic muse, see McClatchy, "Baroque Inventions," 98.

26. For details of Fleming's life with White, see Keith Fleming, *The Boy with the Thorn in His Side: A Memoir* (New York: William Morrow, 2000).

27. Neil Bartlett, "Caracole," *Review of Contemporary Fiction* 16.3 (Fall 1996): 65.

28. Edmund White, *Caracole* (New York: E. P. Dutton, 1985), 49. Subsequent references will be cited in the text.

29. Barber, *Edmund White,* 139.

30. "An Interview with Edmund White," in Brookes, *Gay Male Fiction,* 199.

31. Barber, *Edmund White,* 136.

Chapter Five—Historical Novels

1. Gregory Woods, review of *Hotel de Dream, Chroma: the UK's Only Queer Literary and Arts Journal,* 2 September 2009, http://chromajournal.blogspot.com/2009/09/review-hotel-de-dream-by-edmund-white.html.

2. "Edmund White on Biography, Autobiography, and Fiction," appendix, 127–128.

3. Fulk, "Greece and Homosexual Identity in Edmund White's 'An Oracle,'" 229.

4. Ibid.

5. Purvis, "America's 'White' Cultural and Sexual Dissensus," 310.

6. David Bergman, review of *Fanny: A Fiction, Review of Contemporary Fiction* 23.3 (2003): 128.

7. Purvis, "America's 'White' Cultural and Sexual Dissensus," 313.

8. Elaine Showalter, "Sisters at Odds," review of *Fanny: A Fiction, Guardian Review,* 9 August 2003, 18, http://www.guardian.co.uk/books/2003/aug/09/featuresreviews.guardianreview7.

9. Edmund White, "A Note from the Author," in "P.S.: Ideas, Interviews, & Features included in a new section . . . ," *Fanny: A Fiction* (paperback ed., New York: Ecco Press, 2004), 5.

10. Edmund White, *Fanny: A Fiction* (New York: Ecco, 2003), 4. Subsequent references will be cited in the text.

11. Georgina Lock, review of *Fanny: A Fiction, Cercles: Revue pluridisciplinaire du monde Anglophone,* 2004, http://www.cercles.com/review/r16/white.htm.

12. Edmund White, *Hotel de Dream: A New York Novel* (New York: Ecco, 2007), 224. Subsequent references will be cited in the text.

13. Sophie Gee, "The Red Badge of Scandal," review of *Hotel de Dream*, *New York Times Sunday Book Review,* 16 September 2007, http://www.nytimes.com/2007/09/16/books/review/Gee-t.html.

14. Woods, review of *Hotel de Dream*.

15. Eric Homberger, "An American Tragedy Repainted in Gloss," review of *Hotel de Dream*, *Independent*, 28 September 2007, http://www.independent.co.uk/arts-entertainment/books/reviews/hotel-de-dream-by-edmund-white-464739.html.

16. Henry James, "Letter to Sarah Orne Jewett," 5 October 1901, in *Henry James: Letters, Vol. IV, 1895–1916*, ed. Leon Edel (Cambridge, Mass.: Harvard University Press, 1984), 208.

17. Christopher Benfey, "Outing an Unfinished Novel: Edmund White Takes Liberties with a Stephen Crane Fragment," review of *Hotel de Dream*, *Slate,* 27 August 2007, http://www.slate.com/articles/arts/books/2007/08/outing_an_unfinished_novel.single.

18. Morris Dickstein, "All Made Up: Edmund White Writes the Novel Stephen Crane Never Did," review of *Hotel de Dream,* Bookforum.com (Sept./Oct./Nov. 2007), http://www.bookforum.com/inprint/014_03/847.

19. Eric Karl Anderson, "Dreaming Stephen Crane," review of *Hotel de Dream*, *Gay and Lesbian Review Worldwide* 14.6 (November–December 2007), http://glreview.com/article.php?articleid=34.

20. Compare the narrator's reference to the "hydraulics of passion" in White, *Nocturnes for the King of Naples,* 74.

Chapter Six—Late Works

1. See Edmund Gordon, review of *Jack Holmes and His Friend*, *Sunday* (London) *Times*, 1 January 2012, http://www.edmundwhite.com/html/jackholmes.htm.

2. "Edmund White on Biography, Autobiography, and Fiction," appendix, 128.

3. Edmund White, *Jack Holmes and His Friend* (New York: Bloomsbury, 2012), 391. Subsequent references will be cited in the text. I would like to thank the author for sending me a typescript of his novel, which was not published until the manuscript for this book was nearly complete.

4. Edmund White, *Chaos: A Novella and Stories* (New York: Carroll & Graf, 2007), 53. Subsequent references to this American edition will be cited in the text.

5. Edmund White, *Chaos* (London: Bloomsbury, 2010), 179. Subsequent references to this British edition will be cited in the text.

6. "Edmund White on Biography, Autobiography, and Fiction," appendix, 128.

7. Boyd Tonkin, review of *Jack Holmes and His Friend*, *Independent*, 6 January 2012, http://www.independent.co.uk/arts-entertainment/books/reviews/jack-holmes-and-his-friend-by-edmund-white-6285276.html.

8. See Brian Lynch, "Will and Grace," review of *Jack Holmes and His Friend*, *Irish Times*, 21 January 2012, http://www.irishtimes.com/newspaper/weekend/2012/0121/1224310554379.html.

9. Alex Clark, review of *Jack Holmes and His Friend*, *Guardian*, 20 January 2012, http://www.guardian.co.uk/books/2012/jan/20/jack-holmes-friends-edmund-white-review.

10. White, *A Boy's Own Story,* 170.

Chapter Seven—Biography and Autobiography

1. My interview with White took place at his apartment in New York City on 5 August 2011.

2. See Phillipe Lejeune, *On Autobiography*, trans. Katherine Leary (Minneapolis: University of Minnesota Press, 1989).

3. George Gusdorf, "Conditions and Limits of Autobiography," 1956; rpt. in *Autobiography: Essays Theoretical and Critical,* ed. James Olney (Princeton, N.J.: Princeton University Press, 1980), 43.

4. Paul Robinson, *Gay Lives: Homosexual Autobiography from John Addington Symonds to Paul Monette* (Chicago: University of Chicago Press, 1999), 308.

5. Isabelle de Courtivron, "The High Priest of Apostasy: A Life of Jean Genet, the Renegade Novelist-Playwright Who Cultivated His Legend as a Noble Outlaw," *New York Times Book Review*, 7 November 1993, sec. 7, p. 1.

6. Bertram J. Cohler, *Writing Desire: Sixty Years of Gay Autobiography* (Madison: University of Wisconsin Press, 2007), 3. In this regard, *My Lives*, which White calls an autobiography in the American hardback edition, is retitled a memoir in the American paperback version (2007).

7. Roland Bathes. *Roland Barthes by Roland Barthes*, trans. Richard Howard (New York: Farrar, Straus, Giroux, 1975), 56.

8. Although death from AIDS has been the subject of several significant gay autobiographies, notably Paul Monette's *Borrowed Time: An AIDS Memoir* (San Diego: Harcourt Brace Jovanovich, 1988), Leigh Gilmore notes that skirmishes over the accuracy of autobiographical representations have meant that "not all writers choose autobiography as the mode in which to tell stories of personal pain" (*The Limits of Autobiography: Trauma and Testimony* [Ithaca, N.Y.: Cornell University Press, 2001], 5.)

BIBLIOGRAPHY

Works by Edmund White

Dark Currents. Unpublished novel, 1955. Edmund White Papers. Yale Collection of American Literature, Beinecke Rare Book and Manuscript Library, New Haven, Conn.

The Blue Boy in Black. Unpublished play, c. 1963. Edmund White Papers. Yale Collection of American Literature, Beinecke Rare Book and Manuscript Library, New Haven, Conn..

Forgetting Elena. New York: Random House, 1973. New York: Penguin Books, 1981.

With Charles Silverstein. *The Joy of Gay Sex: An Intimate Guide for Gay Men to the Pleasures of a Gay Lifestyle.* New York: Crown Books, 1977.

Nocturnes for the King of Naples. New York: St. Martin's Press, 1978. New York: Penguin Books, 1980.

States of Desire: Travels in Gay America. New York: E. P. Dutton, 1980.

A Boy's Own Story. New York: E. P. Dutton, 1982. New York: New American Library, 1983.

Caracole. New York: E. P. Dutton, 1985.

With Adam Mars-Jones. *The Darker Proof: Stories from a Crisis.* 1987. New York: New American Library, 1988.

The Beautiful Room Is Empty. New York: Random House, 1988.

Three Times Three (Trios). Unpublished play, nd (produced 1990). Edmund White Papers. Yale Collection of American Literature, Beinecke Rare Book and Manuscript Library, New Haven, Conn.

Genet: A Biography. New York: Alfred A. Knopf, Inc. 1993.

The Burning Library: Essays. Ed. David Bergman. New York: Alfred A. Knopf, Inc. 1994.

With Hubert Sorin. *Our Paris: Sketches from Memory.* New York: Alfred A. Knopf, 1994.

Skinned Alive: Stories. New York: Alfred A. Knopf, 1995. New York: Vintage International, 1996.

The Farewell Symphony. New York: Alfred A. Knopf, 1997.

Marcel Proust. New York: Viking Penguin, 1999.

The Married Man. New York: Alfred A. Knopf, Inc., 2000.

The Flâneur: A Stroll through the Paradoxes of Paris. New York: Bloomsbury, 2001.

Fanny: A Fiction. New York: Ecco, 2003. Paperback ed. New York: Ecco Press, 2004.
Arts and Letters. San Francisco: Cleis Press, 2004.
My Lives: An Autobiography. New York: Ecco, 2006.
Chaos: A Novella and Stories. New York: Carroll & Graf Publishers, 2007.
Hotel de Dream: A New York Novel. New York: Ecco, 2007.
Terre Haute. London: Methuen Drama, 2007.
Rimbaud: The Double Life of a Rebel. New York: Atlas & Co., 2008.
City Boy: My Life in New York During the 1960s and '70s. New York: Bloomsbury, 2009.
Chaos. London: Bloomsbury, 2010.
Sacred Monsters. New York: Magnus Books, 2011.
Jack Holmes and His Friend. New York: Bloomsbury, 2012.

Sources Cited

Adams, Stephen. *The Homosexual Hero in Contemporary Fiction.* London: Vision Press Ltd., 1980.
Anderson, Eric Karl. "Dreaming Stephen Crane." Review of *Hotel de Dream. Gay and Lesbian Review Worldwide,* 14.6 (November–December 2007). http://glreview.com/article.php?articleid=34.
Barber, Stephen. *Edmund White: The Burning World.* New York: St. Martin's Press, 1999.
Bartlett, Neil. "*Caracole.*" *Review of Contemporary Fiction* 16.3 (Fall 1996): 61–68.
———. "The Uses of Monotony: Repetition in the Language of Oscar Wilde, Jean Genet, Edmund White and Juan Goytisolo." In *Flowers and Revolution: A Collection of Writings on Jean Genet,* ed. Barbara Read with Ian Birchall, 113–27. London: Middlesex University Press, 1997.
Barthes, Roland. *Roland Barthes by Roland Barthes,* trans. Richard Howard. New York: Farrar, Straus, Giroux, 1975.
Benfey, Christopher. "Outing an Unfinished Novel: Edmund White Takes Liberties with a Stephen Crane Fragment." Review of *Hotel de Dream. Slate.* 27 August 2007. http://www.slate.com/articles/artsbooks/2007/08/outing_an_unfinished_novel.singl.html.
Bergman, David. *Gaiety Transfigured: Gay Self-Representation in American Literature.* Madison: University of Wisconsin Press, 1991.
———. Review of *Fanny: A Fiction. Review of Contemporary Fiction* 23.3 (2003): 127–28.
———. *The Violet Hour: The Violet Quill and the Making of Gay Culture.* New York: Columbia University Press, 2004.
———, ed. *The Violet Quill Reader: The Emergence of Gay Writing after Stonewall.* New York: St. Martin's 1994.
Bonetti, Kay. "An Interview with Edmund White." *Missouri Review* 13.2 (Summer 1997): 89-110.
Bram, Christopher. *Eminent Outlaws: The Gay Writers Who Changed America.* New York: Twelve, 2012.
Brookes, Les. *Gay Male Fiction Since Stonewall: Ideology, Conflict, and Aesthetics.* New York: Routledge, 2009.

Carlson, Jerry W. "Edmund White's Brilliant New Novel of Sexual Awakening." Review of *A Boy's Own Story. Book Week, Chicago Sun-Times.* 26 September 1982, 27.

Christensen, Peter. "'A More Angular and Less Predictable Way': Epiphanies in Edmund White's *The Darker Proof.*" *Review of Contemporary Fiction* 16.3 (1996): 73–83.

Clark, Alex. Review of *Jack Holmes and His Friend. Guardian,* 20 January 2012. http://www.guardian.co.uk/books/2012/jan/20/jack-holmes-friends-edmund-white -review.

Clum, John M. "'And Once I Had It All': AIDS Narratives and Memories of an American Dream." In *Writing AIDS,* ed. Murphy and Poirier, 200–224.

Cohen, Ed. "Constructing Gender." In *The Columbia History of the American Novel,* ed. Emory Elliott, Cathy Davidson, Patrick O'Donnell, Valerie Smith, and Christopher Wilson, 542–57. New York: Columbia University Press, 1991.

Cohler, Bertram J. *Writing Desire: Sixty Years of Gay Autobiography.* Madison: University of Wisconsin Press, 2007.

Courtivron, Isabelle de. "The High Priest of Apostasy: A Life of Jean Genet, the Renegade Novelist-Playwright Who Cultivated His Legend as a Noble Outlaw." Review of *Genet. New York Times Book Review.* 7 November 1993, sec. 7, p. 1.

Dellamora, Richard. "Apocalyptic Utterance in Edmund White's 'An Oracle.'" In *Writing AIDS,* ed. Murphy and Poirier, 98–116.

Dickstein, Morris. "All Made Up: Edmund White Writes the Novel Stephen Crane Never Did." Review of *Hotel de Dream.* Bookforum.com (Sept./Oct./Nov. 2007). http://www.bookforum.com/inprint/014_03/847.

Dyer, Richard. *The Matter of Images: Essays on Representation.* London: Routledge, 1993.

Edelman, Lee. "The Mirror and the Tank: 'AIDS,' Subjectivity, and the Rhetoric of Activism." In *Writing AIDS,* ed. Murphy and Poirier, 9–38.

Fleming, Keith. *The Boy with the Thorn in His Side: A Memoir.* New York: William Morrow, 2000.

———. *Original Youth: The Real Story of Edmund White's Boyhood.* New York: Green Candy Press, 2003.

Friedman, Alan. Review of *Forgetting Elena. New York Times Book Review,* 25 March 1973, 2–3.

Frontain, Raymond-Jean. "Ardor with a Silent H: Submitting to the Ache of Love in Edmund White's 'Skinned Alive.'" In *The Postmodern Short Story: Forms and Issues,* ed. Farhat Iftekharrudin, Joseph Boyden, Mary Rohrberger, and Jaie Claudet, 144–60. Westport, Conn.: Praeger, 2003.

Fulk, Robert D. "Greece and Homosexual Identity in Edmund White's 'An Oracle.'" *College Literature* 24.1 (February 1997): 227–39.

Gee, Sophie. "The Red Badge of Scandal." Review of *Hotel de Dream. New York Times Sunday Book Review.* 16 September 2007. http://www.nytimes.com/2007/09/16/books/review/Gee-t.html.

Gilmore, Leigh. *The Limits of Autobiography: Trauma and Testimony.* Cornell, N.Y.: Cornell University Press, 2001.

Goldstein, Richard. "Modus Eroticus." Review of *States of Desire: Travels in Gay America. Village Voice,* 28 January 1980, 41–42.

Gordon, Angus. "The Retrospective Closet: Adolescence and Queer Prehistory." *Australian Historical Studies* 36.126 (October 2005): 315–31.

Gordon, Edmund. Review of *Jack Holmes and His Friend*. *Sunday* (London) *Times*, 1 January 2012. http://www.edmundwhite.com/html/jackholmes.htm.

Gusdorf, George. "Conditions and Limits of Autobiography." In *Autobiography: Essays Theoretical and Critical*, ed. James Olney, 28–48. Princeton, N.J.: Princeton University Press, 1980.

Hollinghurst, Alan. "A Prince of Self Approval." Review of *A Boy's Own Story*. *Times Literary Supplement*, 19 August 1983, 875.

Homberger, Eric. "An American Tragedy Repainted in Gloss." Review of *Hotel de Dream*. *Independent*. 28 September 2007. http://www.independent.co.uk/arts-entertainment/books/reviews/hotel-de-dream-by-edmund-white-464739.html.

Hopkins, James. "Degeneration Games." Review of *The Married Man*. *Guardian*, 24 March 2000. http://www.guardian.co.uk/books/2000/mar/25/fiction.reviews1?INTCMP=SRCHDegeneration games.

James, Henry. "Letter to Sarah Orne Jewett," 5 October 1901. In *Henry James: Letters, Vol. IV, 1895–1916*, ed. Leon Edel. Cambridge, Mass.: Harvard University Press, 1984.

Koponen, Wilfrid R. *Embracing a Gay Identity: Gay Novels as Guides*. Westport, Conn.: Bergin & Garvey, 1993.

Kramer, Larry. "Sex and Sensibility." *Advocate*, 734 (27 May 1997): 59–70.

———. "A Personal Appeal." *Reports from the Holocaust: The Making of an AIDS Activist*. New York: St. Martin's, 1989.

Lacan, Jacques. "The Mirror Stage as Formative of the Function of the I as Revealed in Psychoanalytic Experience." In *Écrits: A Selection*, trans. Alan Sheridan, 1–7. New York: W. W. Norton & Co. 1977.

Leavitt, David. Introduction to Fleming, *Original Youth*, xix–xxii.

Lehmann-Haupt, Christopher. Review of *A Boy's Own Story*. *New York Times*, 17 December 1982, C37.

———. "Edmund White's Tale of a Gay Youth." Review of *The Beautiful Room Is Empty*. *New York Times*, 17 March 1988, C29.

Lejeune, Phillipe. *On Autobiography*. Trans. Katherine Leary. Minneapolis: University of Minnesota Press, 1989.

Lock, Georgina. Review of *Fanny: A Fiction*. *Cercles: Revue pluridisciplinaire du monde Anglophone* (2004). http://www.cercles.com/review/r16/white.htm.

Lovell, Chris A. "Remembering Elena: A Review of Criticism of Edmund White's First Published Novel." *Harrington Gay Men's Literary Quarterly* 8.1 (2006): 119–31.

Lynch, Brian. "Will and Grace." Review of *Jack Holmes and His Friend*, *Irish Times*, 21 January 2012. http://www.irishtimes.com/newspaper/weekend/2012/0121/1224310554379.html.

Mathews, Harry. "A Valentine for Elena." *Review of Contemporary Fiction* 6.3 (Fall 1996): 31–42.

McCaffery, Larry, and Sinda Gregory. "Edmund White." In *Alive and Writing: Interviews with American Authors of the 1980s*, 257–74. Urbana: University of Illinois Press, 1987.

McClatchy, J. D. "Baroque Inventions." *Shenandoah* 30.1 (Fall 1978): 97–98.

McRuer, Robert. *The Queer Renaissance: Contemporary American Literature and the Reinvention of Lesbian and Gay Identities*. New York: New York University Press, 1997.

Monette, Paul. *Borrowed Time: An AIDS Memoir*. San Diego: Harcourt Brace Jovanovich, 1988.

Murphy, Timothy F. and Suzanne Poirier, eds. *Writing AIDS: Gay Literature, Language, and Analysis*. New York: Columbia University Press, 1993.

Phillips, Jerry. "Into the Melting Pot: Utopian and Dystopian Themes in Edmund White's *Travels in Gay America*." *Studies in Travel Writing* 1.1 (Spring 1997): 170–98.

Picano, Felice, "Edmund White and the Violet Quill Club." *Review of Contemporary Fiction* 16.3 (Fall 1996): 84–87.

Purvis, Tony. "America's 'White' Cultural and Sexual Dissensus: The Fictions of Edmund White." *Journal of American Studies* 42.2 (2008): 293–316.

Radel, Nicholas F. "Edmund White." In *Dictionary of Literary Biography: American Novelists Since World War II*, 6th series, ed. James and Wanda Giles, 335–51. Columbia, S.C.: Bruccoli, Clark, Layman, Inc., 2000.

———. "(E)racing Edmund White: Queer Reading, Race, and Sexuality in *A Boy's Own Story*." *Modern Fiction Studies* 54.4 (Winter 2008): 766–90.

———. "Self as Other: The Politics of Identity in the Works of Edmund White." In *Queer Words, Queer Images: Communication and the Construction of Homosexuality*, ed. R. Jeffrey Ringer, 175–92. New York: New York University Press, 1994.

Rechy, John. "Together They Stood." Review of *The Beautiful Room Is Empty*. *Washington Post Book World*, April 3, 1988, 4.

Robinson, Paul. *Gay Lives: Homosexual Autobiography from John Addington Symonds to Paul Monette*. Chicago: University of Chicago Press, 1999.

Sedgwick, Eve Kosofsky. *Between Men: English Literature and Male Homosocial Desire*. New York: Columbia University Press, 1985.

Showalter, Elaine. "Sisters at Odds." Review of *Fanny: A Fiction*. *Guardian Review*, 9 August 2003, 18. http://www.guardian.co.uk/books/2003/aug/09/featuresreviews .guardianreview7.

Sontag, Susan. *AIDS and Its Metaphors*. New York: Farrar, Straus, and Giroux, 1989.

Spear, Thomas C. "Edmund White on Queer Autofiction, Biography, and Sidafiction." *a/b: Auto/Biography Studies* 15.2 (Winter 2000): 261–76.

Stambolian, George. Introduction to *Men on Men: Best New Gay Fiction*, ed. George Stambolian, 1–12. New York: New American Library, 1986.

Tonkin, Boyd. Review of *Jack Holmes and His Friend*. *Independent*, 6 January 2012. http://www.independent.co.uk/arts-entertainment/books/reviews/jack-holmes-and -his-friend-by-edmund-white-6285276.html.

White, Edmund. "Edmund White Speaks with Edmund White." *Review of Contemporary Fiction* 16.3 (Fall 1996): 13–20.

———. "The Joy of Gay Lit," *Out* (September 1997): 110–114, 196-197.

———. "A Note from the Author." In "P.S.: Ideas, Interviews, & Features included in a new section. . . ." In *Fanny: A Fiction*, paperback ed. New York: Ecco Press, 2004, 7–10.

———. "Out of the Closet, on to the Bookshelf." In *The Burning Library: Essays,* ed. Bergman, 275–83.

———. "The Personal Is Political." In *The Burning Library,* ed. Bergman, 367–78.

Woodhouse, Reed. *Unlimited Embrace: A Canon of Gay Fiction, 1945–1995.* Amherst: University of Massachusetts Press, 1998.

Woods, Gregory. Review of *Hotel de Dream. Chroma: the UK's Only Queer Literary and Arts Journal,* 2 September 2009. http://chromajournal.blogspot.com/2009/09/review-hotel-de-dream-by-edmund-white.html.

INDEX